PLURALISM

PLURALISM

WILLIAM E. CONNOLLY

Duke University Press

Durham and London

2005

© 2005 Duke University Press

All rights reserved

Printed in the United States of America

on acid-free paper ∞

Designed by Sam Potts Inc.

Typeset in Scala by Keystone Typesetting, Inc.

Library of Congress Cataloging-in-Publication

Data appear on the last printed page of this book.

CONTENTS

ACKNOWLEDGMENTS

I would like to thank the Trustees of the Leverhulme Foundation and the faculty at Exeter University for selecting me for the Leverhulme Professorship I held at Exeter in the fall of 2003. Most of this manuscript was completed at Exeter. Three chapters were presented to the faculty. As a Leverhulme Professor I also gave papers at other universities in England, including the London School of Economics, Essex University, the University of Bristol, and the University of Newcastle. Discussions and debates at these universities were valuable to me in developing this study. A faculty seminar was also organized on "Politics and Time" at Exeter. Its sessions helped me to think further about the central issues in this book. I mention Robin Durie, Will Large, John Dupre, Martin Wood, Tim Dunne, Ian Hampsher-Monk, Jane Bennett, and Regenia Gagnier as colleagues whose participation in the seminar and other discussions was extremely gratifying. We pushed each other to sharpen thoughts that were unclear at first and to take back things that never did become that clear. I would like, above all, to thank Nathan Widder for his admirable work in organizing this seminar, his thoughtful participation in it, and his actions well beyond the call of duty in making me feel at home in Exeter.

I have given versions of these chapters at a national graduate student conference on "Critical Theory in Dark Times" at the University of Minnesota in May 2004, at a meeting of the Japanese Association of American Studies in Kyoto in the summer of 2004, at the Conference on "Experimenting with Intensities" at the University of Trent in May 2004, at the University of California, Berkeley, in the spring of 2002, and at a symposium at Grinnell College on "Modernity and Evil" in the spring of 2001. The ensuing discussions were helpful in sharpening the themes of this book. I note Wendy Brown, Constantin Boundas, Brian Massumi, Rosi Braidotti, Erin Manning, Steve Johnston, Eleanor Kaufman, Daniel Smith, Paul Patton, John Protevi, Kathy Trevenen, Paul Saurette, Fumiaki Kubo, Davide Panagia, Atsushi Sugita, Kathleen Skerrett, and Alan Schrift in particular for insights they provided on these occasions.

Johns Hopkins is a vibrant place to study political theory. Hent de Vries and Paola Marrati in the Humanities Center, Veena Das, Gyan Pandey, and Ruby Lal in the Anthropology Department, Amanda Anderson, Michael Moon, and Jonathan Goldberg in English, and Jane Bennett, Jennifer Culbert, and Dick Flathman in political theory all play important roles in my thinking. Above all, I express appreciation to the graduate students in political theory and allied fields at Hopkins, for the experimental mood and reflective disposition that they bring to seminars. Lars Tonder, Matt Scherer, Matt Moore, Mina Suk, Bhrigu Singh, George Oppel, Simon Glezos, Paulina Ochoa, Smita Rahman, and Nick Tampio are working on related issues; their papers and critical engagements have been illuminating to me. Thomas Dumm and David Campbell kindly read every chapter of this manuscript in an earlier draft. Their commentaries have been extremely helpful to me in crafting the final version. In that respect, I thank Jane Bennett again. A seminar that we taught together at Hopkins on "Time and Politics" finds ample expression in this book, as do the comments she has made on earlier drafts of these chapters.

Two of these chapters were published elsewhere in shorter and different versions. I thank Indiana University Press for permission to reprint in chapter 1 material from "Faith, Territory and Evil," in Alan Schrift, ed., *Modernity and the Problem of Evil* (Bloomington: Indiana University Press, 2004). I also thank Routledge Press for permission to publish in chapter 5 sections from "The Complexity of Sovereignty," in Jenny Edkins and Michael Shapir, eds., *Sovereign Lives: Power in Global Politics* (London: Routledge, 2004), 23–40.

Prelude

Charlie Shin posed severe challenges to a twelve-year-old. This working-class intellectual participated in the sporadic meetings of local union leaders at our house, intervening in a mild voice from time to time to say, "Maybe it's time for Local 598 to unite against capital" and "From each according to his ability, to each according to his need." The other men—now and then a woman participated—would listen politely and then get on with debates about how to win the next union election, expose the latest scam by management, or get the "rank and file" ready for a "wild-cat" strike. Often they would close the meeting by complaining about Walter Reuther, the president of the UAW whom most of them secretly revered. I did not know quite what to make of Charlie. He was the smartest guy in the room, the least imposing physically, the most militant on some issues, the most sensitive and attentive to others, and sometimes a bit out of touch with tactical questions. Charlie was a Marxist by conviction and a pluralist by disposition. He was also, if I recall correctly, the only man in the bunch who could play the piano. His phrases were the ones that stuck.

One day I saw his picture on the front page of the *Flint Journal*.

He had recently been identified as a former member of the Communist Party by the House Un-American Activities Committee. A group of workers had just beaten him up and dumped him on the street in front of the factory gate. Hence the newspaper photo and story. His face had a dazed look, as he was surrounded by toughs whose faces shone with civic virtue. The paper, as I recall, noted the patriotic fervor of the workers. But it also became clear to those close to the scene that many workers in that factory, perhaps a majority, opposed the vigilante action. They were pluralists too. Among them were whites, blacks, Catholics, Protestants, a smattering of Jews, a few atheists. Very few were drawn to Charlie's Marxism. But most respected his disposition, his decency, and his right to work; they wanted to hear his ideas even if they did not endorse them all the way down.

My dad found a lawyer for Charlie, which was difficult under the circumstances. The lawyer's name was Gottlieb, a courageous and noble soul. Our family began going to his brother for our dental work, out of loyalty to the attorney. Unfortunately, the brother was not as good at his craft. But no matter. Charlie soon moved next door to us with his two young daughters; it took a year or two, as I recall, before he regained his job at Fisher Body #2.

I saw Charlie at my dad's funeral decades later. He had driven a few hundred miles to honor his old friend. Charlie is dead now. But if he were to call on the phone today, I would recognize his voice immediately, as you might register the cadence, emotional tone, and distinctive pronunciation of a friend you have not heard from in years. His voice sticks. Its rhythms and resonance expressed his sensibility. My memory of that voice reminds me that political and ethical commitments are composed by models of inspiration and attraction as well as by sound arguments and intellectual exchanges. The two mix together in ways not registered well enough in most contemporary philosophies of ethics and politics.

I suspect that my commitment to pluralism grows in part out of the memory of Charlie's example, mixed in with the response of those workers who helped him survive during the time of troubles. The anxiety that his fate created could have nudged me in a number of directions, I imagine. Toward Marxism, which attracted but did not capture me. Toward a career far from politics. Or toward the bicameral orientation to citizenship that a culture of pluralism secretes and solicits. I wanted Charlie to have a voice in the world, not to be its Voice. Not much danger of the latter, of course. Above all, McCarthyism became real to me the day Charlie found himself on the street in front of that factory gate. A mélange of legislative committees, judicial decisions, press campaigns, organized rumors, FBI investigations, employee blacklists, film plots, vigilante actions, worker anxieties, corporate proclivities, nervous defense lawyers, overweening judges, and subdued academics generated a dark resonance machine much more ferocious than the sum of its parts. Only a minority embraced it. But it permeated the political atmosphere nonetheless. The union movement never recovered its previous glory. My impression, upon entering graduate school several years later, was that the old resonance machine still cast a pall over left-of-center faculty members, even though a large majority of respondents asserted in well-designed polls that it did not.

Pluralists expose and resist such dark resonance machines. But is pluralism too compromised as a general political stance to do the job? Do pluralists, because of the very bicameral structure of their commitments, lack the fervor to defend the condition they embrace? Perhaps pluralism is a philosophy for wimps, for those whose beliefs are too saturated with uncertainty and ambivalence to take definitive action. I don't think so. Charlie was a Marxist, a pluralist, and a sensitive soul with a strong will. My dad was a radical social democrat, and a tough-guy cultural pluralist. His wife, my mother, was a pluralist above everything else. She helped Charlie's daughters during the difficult time; and she often thought and acted against the tide of the day. A bicameral orientation to citizenship was not self-negating in these cases, nor in innumerable others.

Sometimes you hear that the bicameral orientation to citizenship appropriate to pluralism really means relativism. It would be hard to convince innumerable pluralists of that who have put themselves on the line to fight against aggressive, nationalist movements. Bellicose unitarianism is a way of life no pluralist honors, though relativists might be moved to embrace it. Rather, the charge of relativism is the first line of attack advanced by the most aggressive unitarians against pluralism. The accusation does double duty: it drains pluralism of its most attractive qualities, and it vindicates unitarianism as the only alternative to it. At other times you hear that pluralism appeals only to effete élites, academics above all. Ordinary people, it is said, won't tolerate that much ambiguity. Tell that to Charlie, I say, and to workers in Flint who helped restore his job and dignity during a rough time.

The element of truth in this exaggeration, though, is that a bicameral orientation to political life does mean that you keep a foot in two worlds, straddling two or more perspectives to maintain tension between them. A bicameral orientation requires a tolerance of ambiguity in politics, the sort of tolerance that Theodor Adorno in his classic study says is lacking in "the authoritarian personality."[1] There is, first, the faith, doctrine, creed, ideology, or philosophy (I do not distinguish sharply between these) that you adopt as an engaged partisan in the world. Marxism, say. Or a branch of Christianity. Or a particular vision of science. Or Hinduism, Islam, orthodox Judaism, Kantianism, Rawlsianism, neoconservatism, or pragmatism. There is, second, the engrained sense that you should exercise presumptive receptivity toward others when drawing that faith, creed, or philosophy into the public realm. You love your creed; you seldom leave it entirely in the closet when you enter politics. But you appreciate how it appears opaque and profoundly contestable to many who do not participate in it; and you struggle against the tendency to resent this very state of affairs. Pluralists adopt a bicameral orientation to political life. They mix affirmative energies into both sides of that bicameralism. Often, the combination is nourished by a love of the world that overflows the creed embraced in the first instance. It is not necessary to be either an effete intellectual or a hero to adopt a bicameral orientation to politics. A decent respect for the persistent diversity of the human condition suffices.

A lot of things in contemporary life prepare people for the bicameral orientation appropriate to pluralism. Neighborhood life, associational meetings, TV dramas, surprising conversions by friends, relatives, or offspring, new events or movements that bubble into being as if from nowhere, church or temple sermons, interfaith associations, an expansive appreciation of history—the list is almost endless. Indeed, with the impressive acceleration of the fastest zones of culture in contemporary life, it takes massive campaigns stretching from neighborhood crusades through the electronic news media to church indoctrination and police-court actions to turn people against pluralism. McCarthyism was one such campaign in the United States. Some forces in the academy today, fed by right-wing campaigns to cleanse the faculty, would reinstate these pressures. As would the most exclusionary sects in the three religions of the Book and the news reporting on some television channels. The very virulence of these campaigns shows that the bicameral orientation to politics appeals to a significant segment of the populace, distributed across a broad band of gender, class, religious, ethnic, age, and sensual affiliations. While the periodic emergence of a new issue or surprising social movement temporarily throws many for a loop, it takes intensive campaigns by dogmatic constituencies with considerable media, governmental, and corporate power to overturn preliminary dispositions in favor of pluralism. The campaign is often launched by labeling pluralists as relativists, subjectivists, nihilists, or élitists, or merely as self-indulgent. The worry is that such aggressive campaigns are becoming hyperactive again today.

The bicameral orientation to citizenship requires a fair amount of self-cultivation and inter-constituency negotiation to fuel and sustain itself. And the very strength of the cultural predisposition to pluralism in numerous zones of life today mobilizes a series of movements against it.

This book began as an attempt to consolidate ideas about pluralism that I have been developing, in the company of many others, during the last twenty years or so. Each of the previous studies focused on one or two dimensions. I felt a need to pull the parts together. But time keeps rolling. And new issues crystallize. So two dimensions of exploration have been added to the agenda. First, while I have paid attention in the past to the acceleration of pace in late modern life and its intensification of the "politics of becoming," I have not previously attended closely to the relation between the civic virtues appropriate to multidimensional pluralism and the experience of time. Time has now become a central object of inquiry, particularly in chapters 3 and 4. Second, at each historical juncture distinctive threats to order are identified by unitarians to vindicate sharp constraints on diversity. The idea that each regime must be organized around the same religious faith has had a long run. It continues to find ample expression among the opponents of pluralism. This demand is often linked to other nonnegotiable imperatives, such as the security of the state, the integrity of capitalism, the inviolable demands of sovereignty, and the essential unity of a democratic civilization. The cold war generated McCarthyism as an extreme response to threats that the Soviet Union posed to Christian faith and capitalism together. The terrorism of Al Qaeda, in turn, generates new fears, hostilities, and priorities. The McCarthyism of our day, if it arrives, will connect internal state security to an exclusionary version of the Judeo-Christian tradition. So in chapters 1 and 2 I argue that the *expansion* of diversity in faith, within and across states, is good in itself and particularly appropriate to the times.

The other chapters, while touched by these explorations, conform to the initial game plan. The idea is to start with the issue of religion, radiating out to pluralism in multiple zones of life. Multidimensional pluralism I call it, arguing that the expansion of diversity in one domain ventilates life in others as well. We then consider the radical contention that not only human culture but the nonhuman world contains an unruly element of pluralism within it. Chapter 3 explores the contention of William James that the universe itself is marked by a plurality of forces. The universe includes "litter" as one of its components, as well as a plurality of human and nonhuman actors of different degrees of efficacy, whose agency is not entirely reducible to either the lawlike formulas of classical science or the finalist images historically brought against those models. The Jamesian interpretation of the universe meshes well with the Bergsonian image of time presented in the following chapter.

On the partisan side of my bicameralism, I embrace much in the thought of James and Bergson. But as a bicameralist, I also realize that a number of creeds, philosophies, and doctrines can be rendered consonant with pluralism. The critical issue, as we shall see, is the kind of ethos infused into a doctrine or creed. What counts is how the relational dispositions of people blend into the creeds and philosophies that they

embrace and the quality of the institutional ethos of engagement between partisans of different kinds.

A faith, on my reading, is composed of a creed or philosophy plus
the sensibility mixed into it. Bergson and James have faith in powers of
transcendence that I contest. But that faith is expressed in ways condu-
cive to negotiating a positive ethos of engagement between multiple
faiths. James and Bergson enact in their writings the code of bicameralism that they commend to political life writ large.

The importance of sensibility and ethos to creed, philosophy, and
ideology finds some expression in every chapter. But the issue is posed
most actively in chapters 2 and 5. If there is a paradox of sovereignty, as
many theorists contend, the first question to pose is the ethos needed to
negotiate that paradox in ways compatible with democratic pluralism.
The second is to identify the multiple sites of activism open to citizens
who can participate in shaping that ethos. For pluralism is marked not
only by a constitutive tension between the already established pattern of
diversity and the periodic eruption of new constituencies seeking a place
on the register of legitimacy. It is also defined by multiple *sites* of potential citizen action, within and above the state.

At least one pertinent issue is notable by its absence in these pages: the
connection between a culture of multidimensional *pluralism* in which
numerous minorities of different types interact and the reduction of
inequality in the domains of job security, income level, exposure to crime,
health care, retirement programs, environmental risks, and working
conditions. I have presented my position on this question elsewhere and
cannot now think of ways to improve upon it. While some argue that the
achievement of national unity provides the basis from which to reduce
economic inequality, I dissent from this view. Under contemporary conditions of rapid mobility within and between states, the drive to national
unity itself too readily fosters marginalization of vulnerable minorities.
It does so because the rapid pace of late-modern life—the rapid movement of populations, ideas, technologies, identities, and faiths across
generations and territorial borders—works against the realization of the

national imaginary. So when an effort is made to mobilize public support for the reduction of economic inequality, vocal nationalists on the Right argue against these drives on the grounds, first, that many whom they demean would be included among their beneficiaries and, second, that the programs would undermine fixed capitalist principles undergirding the nation. National health care? That would cover welfare recipients, unwed mothers, and (usually in code language) racial minorities. It would also obstruct the free market. The provision of collective goods to help households make ends meet in the domains of transportation, housing, education, and insurance? These policies would subsidize lazy freeloaders in the cities and undermine the untrammeled free enterprise system around which the nation is built.

In the argument between neoconservative and liberal nationalists over equality, the former hold too many cards.

It seems to me that they will continue to do so until we develop the idea of a thick network pluralism that exceeds both shallow, secular models of pluralism and the thick idea of the highly centered nation. Liberal images of the procedural nation are not only *insufficient* in themselves, they tend to collapse under pressure from rightist orientations to the nation that are more thick and dense.

While there are tensions between deep pluralism and the reduction of economic inequality, at a most basic level each sets a condition of possibility for the other. Part of the connection is definitional: an ethos of pluralism extends the issue of equality from economic culture to other cultural identities. But it is also causal, in the sense of that term deployed in this book. To make progress in either reducing economic inequality or extending diversity is to improve the prospects for progress on the other front as well.

I have outlined elsewhere programs to reduce inequality that are compatible with deep, multidimensional pluralism. Those programs focus first and foremost on the public infrastructure of consumption in the domains of health care, transportation, public security, education, housing, and retirement. They make it possible for more citizens to make ends meet by rendering the forms of consumption available more inclusive in character. But on what *common basis*, it will be asked, could citizens in such a diverse state unite behind general programs to reduce inequality? Does it not require a unified consensus to promote such an agenda? If so, that carries us right back to the unity of the nation. Right? Not so. In a culture of multidimensional pluralism, support for the reduction of inequality requires the mobilization of a majority assemblage rather than a unified nation. In such an assemblage, some will support the programs in question out of dire need, some out of this or that material interest central to them, some because they seek to meet moral responsibilities or obligations flowing from this creed or that philosophy inspiring them, some because their loyalty to the assemblage encourages them to concede this issue in exchange for others more dear to them, some because they believe that the long-term effects of inequality increase crime, decrease the quality of democracy, and damage the prospects for cultural diversity, some out of considerations that are primarily aesthetic, and most out of a mixture of these considerations, varying in shape and intensity from case to case and constituency to constituency. Further, some who participate in such a majority assemblage will do so because the program resonates deeply with key elements in their identities, interests, or ethical sensibilities, while others are linked to it in more attenuated ways. The difficulties in forging such a majority assemblage are impressive. No question about that. But the strategic promise of reducing inequality improves if you approach the issue through the lens of multidimensional pluralism rather than that of either national unity or the aggregation of material interests.[2]

A majority assemblage in a culture of multidimensional pluralism is more analogous to a potluck supper than a formal dinner. It is fashioned through a series of resonances between local meetings, internet campaigns, television exposés, church organizations, film portrayals, celebrity testimonials, labor rank-and-file education, and electoral campaigns by charismatic leaders. Multidimensional diversity, inspirational leadership, publicity about the suffering generated by the infrastructure of consumption, micropolitical activity initiated from numerous sites—that is the positive resonance machine to put into motion today.

A distinctive set of intellectuals is interrogated in this study: Augustine, Spinoza, William James, Henri Bergson, Gilles Deleuze, Leo Strauss, Talal Asad, Giorgio Agamben, Michael Hardt, and Antonio Negri, with cameo appearances by Proust, Tocqueville, Nietzsche, Kant, and Rousseau. In several cases I am inspired by the thinker in question; in others, I respond critically. Much of the time inspiration and critical indebtedness blend together, to help me forge an image of pluralist possibility appropriate to intrastate politics and cross-state citizen movements. I am indebted to every thinker on this list, partly for the illumination they provide and partly for the struggles they provoke in me. Most understand that the topics of bicameralism, evil, faith, sensibility, creed, relativism, time, the universe, and sovereignty take on a distinctive appearance when examined through the prism of pluralism. Pluralism is not external to these practices. It infiltrates them, helping to crystallize and compose them. My approach is to introduce a theme in one chapter, and then return to it in a later chapter to fold another dimension into it. Repetition with variation. The hope is to intensify the attraction to pluralism through spiral repetition rather than either bare repetition or presentations insulated from one another.

It has been suggested to me that my commitment to pluralism exudes an aura of optimism when the time itself calls for pessimism. I agree, certainly, that we live in a dangerous time, and that some of the conditions that place pluralism on the agenda harbor tragic possibilities. The promise is stalked by the dangers of economic collapse, nationalist fervor, cultural war, preemptive state wars, nuclear proliferation, religiostate repression, and more besides. These pressures increase the need for pluralism while throwing up roadblocks. The positive agenda could cascade into a negative spiral. But to me, the first task is to convey neither a mood of optimism nor one of pessimism. Both are spectatorial orientations, anchored in the bureaucrat's desire to assess probabilities. The task, rather, is to probe the shape of positive *possibility* in relation to urgent *needs* of the day. Measured by that standard, pluralism provides the most humane and promising agenda to pursue, even as we encounter strong pressures against it. To bypass pursuit of deep, multidimensional pluralism today would be to fail an elemental test of fidelity to the world.

CHAPTER I

PLURALISM
AND EVIL

The Experience of Evil

On 9/11 I heard about the first plane attack while I was in a colleague's office. We did not appreciate its scale at first. After the second plane crashed into the other tower a staff member announced that the university was closed for the day. I felt a crushing need to go home. Riding there on a bike, the horror of it overwhelmed me. I stopped a couple of times to steady myself and to wipe my glasses clean of tears. By the time I reached home images of the first tower collapsing were playing and replaying on CNN. It showed bodies catapulting to the earth. Images of the second collapse soon followed. As the images sank into the visceral register of being, feelings of desolation and uncertainty sank in with them.

Something roughly akin to this had occurred before, during the Cuban missile crisis of 1962, the assassination of President John F. Kennedy, and the killings of Martin Luther King and Bobby Kennedy. The experiences, I say, were comparable, though they were not as devas-

tating. My mind wandered to those earlier events the next day, triggered
no doubt by the trauma the tower attacks had spawned.

I note public events close to home not because they embody the
most horrific instances. The holocausts against Amerindians in the New
World, against Jews, homosexuals, and Romana in Europe, and the devastation wreaked upon the people of Kosovo took more horrific tolls, for
starters. I focus on this set to bring home the link between public recourse to the language of evil and crushing experiences of surprise,
devastation, and uncertainty.

During the Cuban missile crisis no one died, but there was a palpable sense that it might issue in a nuclear conflagration bringing human life on earth to a close. That anxiety was not tied to the conviction
that one agent alone was responsible for the danger. The language of evil
was thus muted, despite the awesome stakes. The danger flowed from an
arms race between two highly armed nuclear states, a race that had spi-
raled out of control. So the experience of tragic possibility overwhelmed
the idea of unilateral evil. The three assassinations, while traumatic,
were not widely accompanied by a sense of the tragic. Those killings
were officially absorbed into the category of crime, though many suspected that such a resolution did not exhaust them. Who are the guilty
parties? How can they be brought to justice? Those were the questions.

The public experience of 9/11 was linked both to the shock accompanying violence against a country that generally treated itself as exempt
from violent attack and uncertainty as to how to characterize the act. A
categorical uncertainty filtered into the heart of the matter, an uncertainty both disclosed and muted by the word "terrorism." The terrorists
were not states; their action was unannounced; they did not use traditional military weapons; they did not attack military targets; and they did
not declare traditional territorial objectives. Yet the event produced a
large number of casualties; it was tied to a struggle of civilizational
proportions; and the nonstate perpetrators defined themselves as enemies of America. The term "terrorism" fills a zone of indiscernibility
between crime within the orbit of a state and war between states. Terrorism is bonded to evil, because of the surprise it engenders, because its
victims are not military agents, because its perpetrators are not recognized as state agents in a world of legitimate states, and because it points

to the insufficiency of the categories of territorial state, international system, war, crime, and justice through which people seek to come to terms with contemporary life.

A world with terrorism is not only more dangerous than many Americans had allowed themselves to believe: it harbors actors and events that unsettle established concepts of territory, faith, law, morality, order, and war. How could a God allow such acts? Should the perpetrators be brought to criminal justice or treated as military opponents? Should we tie them to the states in which they are based? If so, how many states are on the list? Does it include Saudi Arabia, Pakistan, and Palestine? What about Israel, or the United States if its secret operatives engage in assassination plots or undertake actions at odds with international conventions? Should states be treated as unstable nodes of power traversed by a perverse anti-cosmopolitan network that subverts and disrupts the world of territorial states?

Terrorism issues in the lived experience of evil. Evil surprises; it liquidates sedimented habits of moral trust and ordained violence; it foments categorical uncertainty; it originates in a fervent desire to restore closure to a dirempted world; and it generates imperious demands to identify and take revenge on the guilty parties. When you experience evil the bottom falls out of your stomach because it has fallen out of your world. If you have experienced other such traumas, they help to color this one. The accumulation of such events becomes layered into the soft tissues of life, finding expression in both modes of explicit recollection and embodied dispositions to judgment subsisting below the threshold of recollection. Such events teach us about the layered character of being, not as we suffer through them but as we review that suffering.

In thinking about evil it is wise to attend to its phenomenology. For the party, leader, or regime that takes charge of the trauma of evil acquires considerable freedom to mobilize the energies of response in several possible directions. The response might engender new evils, as the American war against Iraq has surely done. And, most dramatically, as the indefinite detention of non-prisoners by the Bush administration at Camp Delta after 9/11 in Guantánamo Bay has done. These detainees were denied legal counsel because they were not accused of any crimes; and yet they were not designated prisoners of war by the Bush regime because they were held on territory by the United States that was alleged not to be under its sovereignty. These noncategorized detainees were placed in a new version of the Gulag; for a long time they were subjected to repeated interrogations, exposed to intense light for twenty-four hours a day, and kept away from inspection or protection by any international agency. They were reduced to what Giorgio Agamben calls "bare life." They were placed in a zone beyond recognized conventions of right and entitlement, either for those accused of crime or for war prisoners. This was done not to identify new ways to protect their dignity while their actions were examined, but to place them outside the purview of state limits, international scrutiny, or publicity.

If a compelling task is to forestall evil it becomes pertinent to work upon ourselves so that we respond firmly to it without perpetuating the phenomenon we seek to expel. But what is evil? Is it a dispensable category in the modern world? An essential one?

The Augustinian Story

A story of evil defines the character, sources, and appropriate mode of response to such experiences of devastation, suffering, and moral shock. A familiar story becomes bonded to the new experience, providing the cultural script through which to respond. There are, however, several such stories. They compete within us as well as between us. The Augustinian story is the most familiar to those growing up within the orbit of Christendom. I focus on that part of the story dealing with responsibility for evil. For that is the script most people in states growing out of Christendom turn to when the bottom falls out of their world. Through this story Augustine seeks not only to identify responsible agents of evil but to ensure that the omnipotent, omniscient, salvational God he confesses is not tainted with any responsibility for it. If the infection were to spread to God the Augustinian story would incline toward the tragic vision he resists.

The first act by Adam was an act of evil freely chosen. The brand-new man, upon receiving an order from his God, was tempted by the new woman to disobey; she in turn had been tempted by the serpent to do so when he posed a simple question to her. Adam nonetheless chose freely to eat of the tree of good and evil when he consented, drawing evil into the world through a free, rebellious act. "The injunction . . . was so easy to observe, so brief to remember; above all, it was given at a time when desire was not yet in opposition to the will . . . Therefore the unrighteousness of violating the prohibition was so much greater, in proportion to the ease with which it could have been observed and fulfilled."[1]

The first act of free will, if you treat merely giving names to animals as below the complexity of willing freely, was an act of disobedience. That act ushers evil into being; it elicits just and severe punishment by the Creator; and it ensures that human beings shall be plagued henceforth by a will divided against itself. The accusation by Jerry Falwell that Americans brought the destruction of 9/11 upon themselves through their secularism and support for homosexuality echoes this story. For Adam and Eve deserved the consequences—the suffering as punishment—visited upon them after that fateful act. Humans, after Adam's act, are divided against themselves; they can henceforth move closer to freedom, virtue, and salvation only by receiving the unfathomable gift of God's grace. If the first rebellion was an act of pure will it was also so inexplicable as to be gratuitous. Indeed evil, on this reading, is gratuitous disobedience to the commands of God (even as Augustine tells a corollary story in which acts of apparent evil contribute to a better world in the future). Evil is freely undertaken; it deserves punishment in proportion to its severity. And human beings, after the fall, are incapable of eliminating it by their own actions alone.

But which *acts* of rebellion are most evil? When people worship a false god or fill the true God with false content they participate in radical evil. When this occurs they themselves are appropriately defined as evil, even though there are limits to the action that other human beings—as opposed to God—can take against them. Consider what Augustine says about the Manicheans, a sect within Christianity to which he once belonged and which he now defines as heresy. The problem with the Manicheans, he writes, is that they translate the two wills contending for hegemony within the human soul into two opposing forces in the world representing two deities, one good and the other evil. The dangerous implication of this translation is that the good God lacks omnipotence, perhaps even the capacity to deliver on the hope of salvation. Augustine came perilously close to this view himself. For he recognized Lucifer as a real being. But he defined him to be a divine creation who fell away from God by his own free will. This account enables Augustine to avoid positing Lucifer as a primordial force in cosmic competition with the benevolent God. So Augustine underlines the precarious difference between the two-world view, and the fall from one world for which Lucifer and Adam are responsible, by defining the first faith to be a manifestation of evil. He could not discern an affirmative power in himself to treat Manicheanism as a contending faith in Christianity with which to enter into a relation of agonistic respect: "Let them perish from before your faith, O God, even as vain talkers and seducers of men's minds perish who detect in the act of deliberation two wills at work; and then assert that in us there are two natures of two minds, one good, the other evil. They themselves are truly evil, when they think such evil things."[2]

"They themselves are truly evil." Augustine is prepared to define carriers of the opposing sect evil even if they take no action against him to stop him from practicing or publicizing his faith. Does the alternative creed unsettle something fundamental to him, perhaps his confidence in a God powerful enough to provide salvation? For the Manichean God, locked in a cosmic struggle, is limited.

There are sore spots in Augustine's own story. They include, first, the question of how this early act by a divinely created human being *could* be untainted by the will of the God who created it and, second, the question of how an omnipotent, omniscient God could both be offended by such actions and know in advance that they must occur.[3] We focus here, however, on a related issue. Against the probable views of Jesus, Augustine helped to consolidate a tradition in which the Universal Church both defines official doctrine and identifies modes of faith to exclude or punish as heresies. While he counseled Christians to obey Caesar in regimes that did not profess Christianity, he felt entitled to pursue a future in which all of civilization professed the truth of Christianity in the same way as he did. This sense of divine entitlement had practical effects, even though Augustine hemmed in those implications to some degree.

Here is what he says in a letter to a pagan who had protested gratuitous violence by vagrant practitioners of Christianity against his people and their sacred places: "You plainly see the Jewish people torn from their abode and dispersed and scattered throughout the whole world . . . , everything has happened just as it was foretold . . . You plainly see some of the temples of [pagan] idols fallen into ruin and not restored, some cast down, some closed, some converted to other uses . . . ; and you see how the powers of this world, who at one time for the sake of their idols persecuted the Christian people, are vanquished and subdued by Christians who did not take up arms but laid down their lives."[4]

"Torn from their abode," "cast down," "idols fallen into ruin." Augustine does not actively condone violence against these inferior faiths, and he elsewhere sets limits to the actions that Christians can take against heretics and pagans. But in adopting the passive voice with respect to these acts of violence, and in failing to counsel corrective action against them, he does sound as though the pagans and the Jews have brought these tribulations upon themselves. He thus takes a first step toward capitulating to what I will call the problem of evil within the very ubiquity and diversity of faith itself.

For me, Augustine's doctrine of divinity, will, grace, universal authority, and evil is too close for comfort to the doctrine of Sayyid Qutb, the radical cleric whose version of Islam is said to inspire Osama bin Laden. Augustine and Qutb disagree on the role and standing of Jesus; they diverge in some of the obligations they sanction to God or Allah. But Qutb, as Roxanne Euben presents his doctrine in *Enemy in the Mirror*, parallels things that Augustine says in the *City of God: Against the Pagans*. Each thinks that only his God is salvational and that salvation is one of the keys to religion as such; each insists that the one true God must eventually be worshiped by all; each claims that the secular world is tainted with corruption; each claims that there are clear, undeniable truths of revelation applicable to all humans; each calls those who deviate from the true faith heathen and pagans; and each uses such claims and admonitions to bolster the authority of the church embraced. The heathen for Augustine were Greeks and Romans who denied the Christian God; in the Middle Ages they become Islamists and, later yet, the new pagans in America. For Qutb they are, first, Jews, Christians, secularists, and rationalists who forsake the true God and, second, those within Islam who wander from pure Islamic faith. Here are a couple of formulations from Qutb:

> The purpose of the righteous guidance is the good and prosperity of humanity: the good that springs from the return of mankind to its Creator; the prosperity that emanates from the congruence between the movement of humanity and . . . the noble stature that God intends, freed from the dominance of desires.
>
> When the highest authority is God alone—and is expressed in the dominance of divine law—this sovereignty is the only kind in which humans are truly liberated from slavery to men. Only this is "human civilization," because human civilization requires that the basis of rule be the true and perfect freedom of man.[5]

Let me be clear about the scope and limits of the parallels. I do not say that Augustine and Qutb are the same, or even that Augustinianism takes the first step on a road that *necessarily* leads to Qutbism. Augustine acknowledged more human limits than Qutb does—in limiting the degree of human repression against those defined as pagans or heretics. Moreover, just as Augustine is not reducible to Slobodan Milosevic in his war against Islamists in Kosovo, Qutb is not reducible to Osama bin Laden. I do suggest, however, that what might be called the temptation to evil within faith circulates within both confessions. It is the tendency to define your faith as absolutely authoritative for others, and to treat it as under severe assault or even persecution until it is confessed by everyone with whom you interact. The temptation of Augustinianism and Qutbism is that it is all too easy to define those outside the faiths as evil. To succumb to that temptation is to take a fateful step toward either enacting or tolerating violence against others who do not otherwise threaten your life, your livelihood, or the ability to observe your faith in the company of other believers.

The Augustinian problem of evil revolves around how to locate responsible human agents of evil in a world created by an omnipotent,
benevolent, salvational God innocent of it.[6] Another problem of evil,
however, entangled in the ubiquitous, visceral experience of faith itself,
is how to embrace your faith ardently without acting forcefully to punish,
correct, exclude, or terrorize those who interact with you and contest it.
The problem of evil within faith, as I will call it, is not confined to
Augustinianism and Qutbism. Atheists are capable of it, too. It thus
operates more generally in a world where there is never a vacuum in the
domain of faith. The problem of evil within faith does not necessarily
flow from any particular creed or doctrine of faith alone. The *sensibility*
infusing carriers of the creed is highly pertinent. It exerts an effect upon
the degree to which they feel besieged by "unbelievers" or "the faithless"—that is, by those who practice different existential faiths but who
do not threaten their lives or stop them from practicing their own. In this
respect, Augustine is more moderate than Qutb, and the Islamic moderate, rationalist, and mystic Muhammed 'Abduh is more moderate than
both of them.[7] All three tower above Osama bin Laden and Milosevic.
But perhaps none has come to terms sufficiently with the tendency to
evil inhabiting faith itself in a world where faith is ubiquitous to life and
people persistently embrace a variety of faiths.

The Spinozist Story

An alternative story finds one spiritual anchor in Baruch de Espinoza,
the young man expelled from Judaism by the Elders of Amsterdam in
the seventeenth century and yet labeled a "Jewish philosopher" by many
Christian philosophers and scientists who encountered his work. Bene-
dict Spinoza, as he renamed himself, thus experienced the ugly side of
the passions of faith firsthand. He also knew Hebrew, the language in
which the book of Genesis was written. He concluded, before it was
established more closely by modern scholars, that the book was patched

together from several sources. He may have been drawn to what is now called the "J version," the earliest draft, written in sparse and sweeping prose.[8]

While Augustine reads much of Genesis literally, with only those passages inconsonant with the salvational doctrine of his Church to be read allegorically, while Qutb seeks to follow the divine words of Al-Qur'an exactly, Spinoza asserts that the Bible is best read allegorically. It is taken literally only by children and simple people inducted into the lower levels of ethical life. "I say," Spinoza writes, "that Scripture, being particularly adapted to the needs of the common people, continually speaks in merely human fashion, for the common people are incapable of understanding higher things."[9] If the allegory is taken literally it can contribute to evil: that is, to quick attributions of pure evil against those who diverge from the details of your reading and faith, and to violent energies of revenge against them disguised as just punishment for infidelity.

Read allegorically, however, Genesis helps people to climb above the crude morality of law, will, and punishment of diversity toward a higher ethic of cultivation. Such an ethic is grounded in intellectual love of the complexity of being and infused with the presumptive tolerance of a variety of faiths. It encourages you to recraft the model of morality as law into a complex ethic of cultivation. It further encourages you to open up public space for this image of ethics to attain legitimacy as one possible orientation to ethical life, even while it also counsels tolerance of those who persist in the idea of morality as law.[10] Here is how Spinoza interprets the highest reading of the oldest version of Genesis at a critical juncture: "Therefore the command given to Adam consisted solely in this, that God revealed to Adam that eating of that tree brought about death, in the same way that he also reveals to us through our natural understanding that poison is deadly. If you ask to what end he made this revelation, I answer that his purpose was to make Adam that much more perfect in knowledge."[11]

It was necessary to eat from the tree of knowledge to learn that humans are mortal, but the experience of having the scales lifted from your eyes is like eating poison. The simple couple began to hallucinate upon eating the fruit. And the bottom fell out of Eden. Under the effects of this hallucination they *retrospectively* interpret their action as an act of free disobedience to divine law, and the consequences issuing from it as just punishment delivered to them by Yahweh. So while Augustine interprets death to be just punishment visited on humanity after Adam's sin, to Spinoza it is a part of life itself that preexists action. While Augustine holds Adam primordially responsible for disobedience to a divine command, Spinoza denies primordial responsibility, saying that the idea of responsibility emerges as a secondary formation treated as if it were primary. It is one thing to affirm responsibility as an adult, another to assume that you are primordially responsible for evil in the world.

The Augustinian and Qutb stories would be read by Spinoza as reversals of the human condition recited under the experience of suffering and duress. They are retrospective inversions, something like the one we experience when we think after the fact that we have jumped away from a hot stove because we felt pain, when in fact we responded to a lightning-fast infra-percept before the feeling of pain arrived.

That is why it is important to keep the phenomenology of evil before us. For on Spinoza's reading, when the bottom falls out of your world you are apt to become flooded with the desire to find parties to accuse of pure evil. You become sorely tempted to revenge against them, by-passing the question of whether the action you take will help to avoid having the experience recur in the future or rather exacerbate the cycle of violence already under way. You are incited to become a carrier of the thing you condemn.

Spinoza eschews the language of evil itself because he finds it tied too closely to the ideas of a commanding God, primordial guilt through free will, and a theological justification of base human drives to revenge. He thinks the term cuts too strongly against an ethic that grows out of joy in the complexity of existence amid the considerable suffering that life brings to embodied, mortal beings. But is it possible to retain the sense of suffering and despair attached to the experience of evil while contesting its *necessary* attachment to the first set of ideas? For they express one contestable faith rather than the sole necessary or unavoidable faith; they express a type of faith with which many are imbued but not the type that everyone must confess in order to be worthy of being treated like a dignified human being. I am drawn to such a combination: to retain the language of evil in order to identify the most horrible and devastating actions taken by some human beings against others; and to disconnect evil from *necessary* implication in the Augustinian story of it. To define something as evil, now, is to respond to the trauma of evil and to support reflective action to forestall it in the future. At the same time, to disconnect evil from necessary involvement in one faith alone is to open the door to combat what I am calling the temptation to evil inside the fabric of faith itself in a world in which faith is ubiquitous. It is to maintain appreciation of the role that faith plays in human life while encouraging creative exploration of how multiple faiths—including both theistic and nontheistic faiths—can coexist privately *and* publicly on the "same strip of territory," to use a phrase of Spinoza's.

The Spinoza story, once this adjustment has been made, can be seen to contain difficulties of its own. How certain can one be of *his* philosophy of univocal substance? Is it a demonstrated philosophy or one permeated with contestable faith? What is to be done with, or to, those who insist upon correcting or punishing others based upon their ("literal") readings of Scripture, even when the others do not threaten their lives or the possibility of practicing their faiths? How and when does a Spinozist attribute responsibility for violent acts? These difficulties, in my view, correlate with a corresponding set in the stories that Spinoza contends against: How stable and steady, anyway, is the Augustinian notion of responsibility through free will, particularly after the human will is said by him to have become divided against itself, humans are said to be plagued by original sin, and freedom and salvation are said to depend more upon the grace of God than self-caused action by the faithful?

It is the confidence with which Spinoza asserts his basic philosophy-faith, and the dismissive way he sometimes responds to those who differ from it, that requires more attention. He does not anathematize other faiths strongly, and he does call for tolerance of numerous faiths in the same regime. Still, he has inordinate confidence in the certainty of his philosophy; and his support of tolerance flows from the majestic sense that the demonstrable truth of his philosophy is unavailable to the multitude who live at the level of passion and superstition rather than reason and joy in the complexity of being. Consider, on this note, the engagement between Spinoza and a former follower who wrote to him from

Florence in 1675 to announce his conversion to Catholicism. Alfred Burgh besought Spinoza to do the same. Burgh's letter is severe, accusing Spinoza of atheism, pride, and arrogance, invoking the authority of Augustine against pagans, atheists, and heretics, pointing to the unbroken tradition of Catholic faith as a sign of its truth, and promising Spinoza a hot place in hell if he does not repent. One of Spinoza's sins was that he was a "philosopher." "Come to your senses, philosopher, acknowledge the folly of your wisdom, and that your wisdom is madness. Practice humility instead of pride and you will be healed. . . . Consult Catholics who are deeply learned in their faith . . . and they will tell you many things that you have never known and that will amaze you."[12]

Spinoza responds a few months later. In the midst of rebutting Burgh's reading of Scripture, reminding him that Judaism has a longer heritage of unbroken faith than Catholicism, and chastising him for omitting from his list of blessed believers "Lutherans, the Reformed Church, the Mennonites and the Enthusiasts, to say nothing of others," Spinoza writes, "Still you appear to be willing to resort to reason, and you ask me 'how I know that my philosophy is the best of all those that have been taught in this world, are now being taught, or will ever be taught in the future.' But surely I have far better right to put that question to you. For I do not presume that I have found the best philosophy, but I know that what I understand is the true one. If you ask me how I know this, I reply that I know it in the same way that you know that three angles of a triangle are equal to two right angles. That this suffices no one will deny who has a sound brain and does not dream of unclean spirits who inspire us with false ideas as if they were true. For truth reveals both itself and the false."[13]

The courage of Spinoza is not in doubt. He had been anathematized, with some noble exceptions, by Christians, Jews, and secular rulers; his ideas and texts had been driven underground; a former teacher had been hanged; other friends and allies had been imprisoned; and he himself was a marked man. Burgh, for his part, had become a favorite of the Church in Italy and was soon to join the Inquisition.[14] Every nontheist has faced a Burgh or two, even though the immediate stakes are not always so high. But as one attracted to Spinoza's ideas of philosophical monism, immanent causation, religious tolerance, and an ethic inspired by joy in the complexity of being, I am nonetheless disconcerted by his reply. He meets Burgh's insistence upon the universal authority of the Catholic faith with a reply that recapitulates its logic. This philosopher, who counseled a more wide-ranging tolerance than any other thinker of the day of whom I am aware, nonetheless meets the insistent assertion of universal faith with confident certainty in the self-sufficient power of general reason. He is certain of a correspondence between the logic of geometry and the structure of the world. That confidence, in turn, is encouraged by his conviction that faith in a personal God is lodged in the imagination, and that the imagination consists of crude, inflamed ideas operating below the clarity and joy of reason.

Spinoza, the preeminent philosopher of the radical Enlightenment, and Burgh, a born-again Catholic, instigate a logic of mutual castigation that continues, with numerous variations, relaxations, and intensifications, into the present. The combatants together divide theology from philosophy, science from faith, and reason from imagination, though there are resources within Spinoza's philosophy that could loosen the last division. And this pattern of engagement persists after them. Kant, for instance, gives it a new spin a century later, when he combats the "dogmatism" of ecclesiastical faith with certainty in the "unity of reason" and the necessary postulate of a moral God that it secretes. Kant exudes confidence that his new concepts of theoretical, practical, and aesthetic reason set definitive limits to ecclesiastical authority and demonstrate the falsity of Spinozist reason. His articulation sets the stage for the modern, secular division between private faith and public reason.

What if Spinoza, in that early exchange, had confessed *faith* in a correspondence between geometry and the structure of the world? What if he had asserted that he could offer impressive evidence and arguments in support of his faith, but that he was not yet in a position to inform those invested with Christian or Jewish faith that they were surely mistaken on the most critical points? If so, he and others of similar belief might still have been anathematized by many Christians and Jews of that day, including prominent Cartesian philosophers, physicists, and mathematicians. *But he might have opened a window to future negotiation of a different kind of relation between devout partisans of disparate faiths and philosophies.* He would also have put philosophy and religion on the same plane, rather than joining future philosophers and theologians alike in putting them on different planes while disagreeing over which plane is higher. He would have pointed out the pertinence of evidence and argument to religion and faith, and the role that faith plays in philosophy. And he would have taken a step toward initiating the politics of agonistic respect already whispering within this early, republican ideal of politics, replacing the majesty of tolerance bestowed by the authoritative center upon minorities with a politics of restrained contestation and selective collaboration between alternative philosophy-faiths. These philosophy-faiths would be linked less by common points of certainty and more by the reciprocal modesty induced by their joint inability, so far, to demonstrate the truth of their respective commitments to those not already inducted into them. Spinoza would thus have taken a giant step toward combating the problem of evil within faith.

Existential Faith and Evil

By existential faith I mean an elemental sense of the ultimate character of being. That sense is typically shared with others, albeit often incompletely and imperfectly. It finds expression in organized institutions. In Euro-American states it often—but certainly not always—revolves around belief in a personal God. And it is not completely exhausted by the pile of beliefs that its adherents profess. An existential faith does find expression on the epistemic field of doctrine and belief, but its intensities extend below that field as well. It thus has a *horizontal dimension*, in that its beliefs about such issues as divinity, morality, and salvation are professed and refined through comparison to alternative beliefs advanced by others. And it has a *vertical dimension*, in that the doctrinal element is confessed and enacted in ways that express embodied feelings, habits of judgment, and patterns of conduct below direct intellectual control. The institutionalization of faith reaches the lower registers of affect-imbued ideas as well as those operating at a more refined level of reflection. When your faith is disturbed your being is rattled. You react bodily through the roiling of your gut, the hunching of your shoulders, the pursing of your lips, and the tightening of your skin. The visceral dimension of faith, moreover, bubbles into explicit belief, affecting the intensity with which you respond to debates about elemental questions. The relation moves the other way too: a crisis of belief might lead you to adopt exercises to modify the visceral register of faith. There is, then, a fugitive *circuit* in play between visceral faith and explicit belief, a circuit in which each element becomes incorporated enough into the other that the relation between them cannot be parsed into a simple pattern of cause and effect.

To be human is to be inhabited by existential faith. There is no vacuum in this domain, though there might very well be ambivalence, uncertainty, and internal plurality. On this reading there is no constituency that is simply faithless. "Faithlessness" is typically a demeaning term that proponents of some faiths give to other faiths that assault their own sense of universality. Less often it is a term of self-description by those who have broken with the dominant faith in their neighborhood and conclude that they have broken with faith per se. Scientists and secularists, however, do not simply live "above faith." Each contemporary scientist draws an element of faith into his or her craft, even when it is tied to closely specified regimes of evidence. It might be the faith— as we shall see in chapter 3 when William James challenges the self-certainty of this faith—that the world conforms in the last instance to laws articulable in principle by human beings.

A religious faith, moreover, is not entirely reducible to that fugitive experience of difference, or the oblivion of being, or remainders beyond meaning, invaluably explored by Heidegger, Levinas, and Derrida.[15] The oblivion of being may well subsist as a disruptive dimension within an existential faith. But each faith inflects this experience in a specific way. It makes considerable difference to your life whether you confess that Jesus is the Savior; or that God grants eternal salvation to some through His unfathomable grace; or that morality takes the form of divine laws we are obligated to obey; or that it is imperative to pray every day while facing Mecca; or that the gods do not worry about affairs of this world.

One sign of the obdurate facticity of faith is how some intellectuals who honor the oblivion of Being attach the name "God" to it while others speak at that moment of a "swarm" of virtual differences without divinity. Each expression is punctuated by an idea of difference, but it is inflected differently in each case. Faith, on my reading, is ubiquitous, even as it is punctuated by that which exceeds its doctrinal form. Moses, Buddha, Jesus, Paul, Augustine, Mohammed, Spinoza, Newton, Qutb, 'Abduh, Nietzsche, Emmanuel Levinas, Albert Einstein, Jon Elster, and John Rawls are all inhabited by existential faiths; and each investment makes a difference to the public doctrine enunciated by each and how life is lived in relation to that doctrine.[16] That's why I do not make the sharp distinction between religious faith and secular reason, or theology and philosophy, that many secular philosophers and some theologians make (though not Nietzsche, Kierkegaard, Bergson, James, Derrida, Deleuze, or Levinas).

The problem of evil *within* faith flows from the dissonant conjunction between the *layering of faith* into the body-brain circuits of the faithful and the *relational character of faith* in a world marked by numerous faiths. A specific faith indeed *requires* other faiths to be; that is, it requires an array of different faiths to provide it with needed contrasts through which to demarcate itself.[17] But the publication of those alternative faiths, needed for the specification of yours, can also threaten self-confidence that your faith expresses the essence of being. *It is inside this double constitution of faith itself that the problem of evil within faith is insinuated.* I suspect that every faith is haunted by a potential for madness; that potential is tapped when its visceral trust is stalked by actions that strike it as blasphemy or sacrilege.

The tendency to evil within faith is this: The instances in which the faith of others incites you to anathematize it as inferior or evil can usher into being the demand to take revenge against them for the internal disturbance they sow, even if they have not otherwise limited your ability to express your faith. Again, the potential for madness in faith is activated not only by the threats that other faiths pose to our lives or possibilities of expression. It also arises when their ardent confessions honor a source of morality at odds with the one we construe to be universal, or challenge our demand to dominate public space. Augustine, Qutb, Milosevic, and Osama bin Laden all display this tendency to evil within faith, to different degrees. Spinoza, on the other hand, takes one step away from it and another toward it. The more relentless the drive to universalize an existential faith, the more its supporters experience otherwise tolerable differences to be forms of persecution demanding reprisal.

Faith is ubiquitous, relational, and layered into body-brain-culture circuits, for good and ill. It provides us with sustenance and vigor, and it can incite implacable revenge against those whose mode of being assaults its self-confidence. The double situation of faith generates the temptation to evil within it. That temptation is not sufficiently modulated through the practice of secularism, in which diverse faiths are shuffled into the private realm so that a matrix of public reason free of any particular faith can operate in the public realm. Secularism constitutes a noble attempt to respond to the problem of evil within faith. But secularists themselves very often have inordinate faith in the self-sufficiency of the public procedures they endorse. And in the corollary idea that faith can be left at home as you enter the public arena. They also underplay the ubiquitous role of ritual and technique in shaping the visceral register of political culture. Euro-American secularists typically overplay the autonomy of public reason (or whichever surrogate for it is adopted), underplay the layering of faith into bodies and institutions, and discount the extent to which the concepts of free will, punishment, and public morality that they deploy express the history of the Christendom in which they participate.[18]

Territorial Unitarianism and Evil

In an age when the acceleration of speed in several domains compresses distance—increasing the number of disparate faiths inside each territorial state and intensifying the interaction between them—one tempting way to respond to the problem of evil within faith is to pursue a line of correspondence between the constitution of a territorial state and the institutional organization of faith. Hobbes, Rousseau, and Tocqueville pursued such a resolution, in different ways, with Tocqueville saying that the unity of Christianity provides the first political institution of America. Several Christian evangelists, Islamic clerics, and supporters of Israel as a Jewish state do much the same. But such a strategy exacerbates the potential for evil within faith. The agenda generates refugees, repressed minorities, diasporic peoples, or worse in its wake.

And it cannot be generalized across states. The key fact of the late modern time is that there is not enough contiguous land for every religious "people" (broadly or narrowly defined) to secure a politically organized strip of territory for itself alone. The most fundamental objection, not to the territorial state, but to a world of territorial *nation*-states composed of religiously unified peoples, is this: the religiously unified territorial nation is no longer a universalizable form, if it ever was. For every "people" to "own" a land, and consolidate a state, you would have to erect huge multilevel garages on the face of the earth, stacking territories so there would be enough bounded land for each people. Many would not receive much sun. Then you would have to organize massive migrations, seeking a new place for each minority on a globe without unoccupied areas. Perhaps the attraction of the *Star Wars* films is the fantasy of finding such virgin territory somewhere. Even hybrid faiths, of innumerable sorts, would require separate garage space. And these multifarious migrations would then have to be ratified by limitations upon intermarriage, travel, tourism, international communications, and economic intersection, so that new forces of connection, hybridization, and becoming would not coalesce. To maintain such a world order it would then be necessary to slow time to a snail's pace, which helps to explain why so many devotees of the territorial *nation*-state are captured by the utopian fantasy of slowing the world down.

The religiously unified nation-state—organized around generic categories such as Christianity, Judaism, Buddhism, Islam, or Hinduism or more specific categories within these forms—is simply not a universalizable form.[19] The relentless pursuit of territorial unitarianism therefore spawns persecution, forced conversions, refugees, boat people, terrorism, ethnic cleansing, and worse. It spawns evil, even when its proponents do not directly seek evil. So the fantasy of territorial unitarianism intensifies rather than resolves the potential for evil within faith. This fact either makes the pursuit of deep pluralism an ethical necessity within politically organized territories or sets up future violence on behalf of territorial unitarianism that will make the American holocaust against Amerindians seem like an early shot in an endless series of civil wars.

Faith and Its Relations

To address the obdurate problem of evil within faith while respecting the ubiquity of faith we need a model of deep pluralism that reaches beyond the agenda of territorial unitarianism as well as that of shuffling faith into the private realm. Our engagement with the problem of evil within faith, then, begins to make the case for the idea of multidimensional pluralism, to be pursued in chapter 2.

I do not deny that a specific historical condition can present a compelling case for constituting special spaces of territorial sovereignty. The conquest of aboriginal peoples in the settler societies of the United States, Australia, Canada, and New Zealand provides such a series of instances.[20] Nor do I forget that other historical circumstances mean that pluralism should sometimes be pursued cautiously. The quest to end the bloodshed in the Middle East, for instance, may require militant cross-state citizen activism on behalf of a contiguous state of Palestine, joined to international support for the maintenance of Israel. But this agenda must also be pursued in a way that supports the promise of future pluralism within each state. Moreover such religiously anchored modes of territorial sovereignty should be understood as the exception rather than the rule, to be supported only under extreme situations of duress.

Some strains within gay and lesbian movements provide valuable pointers here. Many gay and lesbian activists, for instance, press in favor of a positive pluralization of sexual and gender identities on the same territory.[21] The successful enactment of such plurality, moreover, involves a micropolitics of self-modification in the relational identities of straights, in which they cultivate a bicameral orientation to their own practices of sensuality. You enact your sexual affiliation as if it were the natural way of being; but, in another gesture, you come to terms, viscerally and reflectively, with the extent to which it is neither the natural nor the universal form of sexuality. This agenda once seemed impossible to many. But in the interests of abetting sexual plurality, numerous straights have worked on themselves tactically, rendering the visceral sense that their sexuality is the only natural mode amenable to second-order correction.

Intellectualism, in this domain, is pertinent but insufficient to the issue. For avoidance of the problem of evil in faith often *involves acceptance of some risk to the stability of your own identity.* That is what makes the cultivation and negotiations involved here ethico-political rather than, say, reducible to a judgment of tolerance located on the highest intellectual register alone. The oscillation back and forth between work on our relational selves and work on others can be abetted by films and TV dramatizations that combine image, voice, sound, and rhythm to work on the visceral register of being. For it is through such passive syntheses of sensory experience that our sensual orientations were composed in the first place. I would cite *Northern Exposure* and *Six Feet Under* as affirmative examples of such a micropolitics in action. They open people viscerally to the risks and pleasures of diversity.

Given the violent, self-defeating character of territorial unitarianism, the most promising way to respect the depth, ubiquity, and diversity of faith without falling into the potential for evil inhabiting it is to encourage practitioners in each practice of faith to cultivate a bicameral orientation to their own faith. This is where traces inside your faith that exceed its creedal dimension can become productive. You cultivate your faith in the company of others in the first instance. You then come to terms empirically with the variety of faiths and the impossibility of generalizing territorial monism peacefully in a world marked by such plurality. You participate, both individually and within your faith community, in artful exercises and rituals to mix an element of relational self-modesty and presumptive generosity inside your faith. You are motivated do so, again, to ward off the potential for evil within the layering of faith. Finally, you work politically to negotiate a generous ethos of engagement between multiple faiths whose participants inevitably bring pieces and chunks of it with them into the public realm.

In a multicultural world, such a double orientation to the ubiquity of faith is the best antidote to the potential for evil within the compass of faith. It is comparable to the double consciousness attained when people correct their perceptual sense that the sun rotates around the earth with second-order knowledge that the reality is the other way round. It is, I say, comparable to such a familiar double-entry orientation, though not entirely reducible to it. In each case you may need to repeat tomorrow the modification enacted yesterday, until the correction itself becomes more or less automatic. And it is true that in the Middle Ages the idea that the sun moved around the earth was crucial to the self-understanding of Christianity. But that has changed. Today, however, existential faith remains invested with the judgment that it somehow expresses a fundamental truth of being. It is here that things become tricky. But another difference between existential faith and our example of the sun and the earth saves the day. It is not necessary that you treat your faith in the second movement to be uncertain to you—though some admirable believers seek to do just that. You merely need to come to terms viscerally and positively with the extent to which it must appear profoundly *contestable* to others inducted into different practices, exposed to different events, and pulled by different calls to loyalty.

Suppose you are a neuroscientist, predisposed by training and disposition to treat the world as matter in motion all the way down. You think faith in a God to be a form of superstition. It may be pertinent now to recall experiments by other neuroscientists that explore the body-brain patterns of believers as they are in the very midst of mystical experience. These experiments do disclose an interesting set of body-brain patterns. You may even participate in such experiments, placing a piece of your faith at modest risk in the interests of engaging, albeit very imperfectly, an element in the faith of others pertinent to appreciating the contestability of your own faith.[22] You may now find it more understandable that some will link such fugitive experiences to mystical illumination while you interpret them as earthy attachments that enter into your love of material complexity. Different tactics of self-intervention, of course, are appropriate to different constituencies, depending upon the shape of their faith and the specific relations in which it is set. The effort is first, to get a whiff of experiences heretofore alien to you; second, to come to terms positively with how and where your faith feels strange to those immersed in different regimes of ritual, creed, scientific experiment, awakenings, and defining historical events; and third, to work tactically on yourself and others to overcome existential resentment of this persistent condition of human being.

As you cultivate this second-order sense, it begins to sink into the visceral register that promotes conduct on its own and also flows into conscious beliefs and judgments. The correction now becomes both more automatic and more refined. This light recoil upon the relational dimension of your own faith is embraced in order to become more ethical in a fast-paced world. It is part of the process by which the ritual dimension of faith is appreciated even as the civic virtues of deep pluralism are folded into this relational practice. The motive to pursue such a path grows in part out of that moment of rupture within your own faith, in part out of the hospitality toward others that forms part of your faith, in part out of the desire to avoid being a victim of persecution yourself, and in part out of appreciation of the contemporary condition in which a variety of faiths coexist on the same politically organized territory. These multiple sources, at their best, feed each other, amplifying each other.

The relational modulation of faith, again, inserts an element of agony into faith. Something is received in return: You sacrifice the demand for the unquestioned hegemony of your faith to curtail the occasions when its very defense calls upon you to impose otherwise unnecessary violence or suffering on others. You accentuate a dimension of your faith: its call to tolerance unless it is subjected to intolerable provocation. You do so, however, by recomposing *what counts* as an intolerable provocation to your faith.

Installation of a bicameral orientation to the relational dimension of your own faith is never entirely attained. When you pursue such a program, old flames of anathematization will periodically flare up again, and new and unexpected movements of faith by others will arise to pose the issue all over again in surprising terms. Such a double perspective is fostered by religious work, individual and collective. It juxtaposes exercises of the self to a positive version of the micropolitics by which we regularly work on each other. That is, it involves the essence of ethicopolitical life in a pluralistic society.

The most basic problem of political ethics, on this view, is not how to get participants to obey a universal moral source that they already profess in common. This is an issue that concerns Augustine, Rousseau, Kant, Tocqueville, and Qutb, in different ways. It is a difficult issue. But we do not live in a time when most politically organized territories are populated by people who share one fundamental religious faith *or* one source of public morality. Even states said to be Hindu, Buddhist, Jewish, Christian, Islamic, or secular contain significant minorities who do not confess those faiths. They are also populated by large numbers of the faithful who are not as pure as the most ardent devotees think they should be. Thus a basic challenge of ethico-political life in late modern territorial states is how to negotiate honorable public settlements in settings where interdependent partisans confess different existential faiths and final sources of morality. When that is acknowledged as a basic challenge of territorial politics, and when shallow secular conceptions of diversity are recognized as providing an insufficient response to this condition, our attention turns to the task of forging a positive ethos of engagement between multiple constituencies coexisting on the same strip of territory. It turns, above that, to the question of how to instill such an ethos into cross-state citizen actions designed to limit the evils that states do to each other. The most basic questions of ethics are therefore ethico-political, because the participants do not have recourse to either a single source of existential sustenance or a set of procedures sufficient to the issues in question. The most basic ethico-political questions impinge upon those circuits flowing back and forth across the visceral and reflective dimensions of culture.

I noted earlier that in addressing faith it is wise to pay attention to the circulation between the *creed* professed by a constituency and the *sensibilities* of those who profess it. The two elements are not neatly separable, for the sensibility with which you are endowed inflects the creed. And vice versa. It is nonetheless pertinent to work on the sensibility infused into your faith. For instance, you might resist the doctrines of evil posed by Augustine and by Qutb. But then recall how such thought-imbued passions surge up in you too when the bottom drops out of your world. It may seem wise now to engage these creeds as contestable faiths, coming to terms publicly with historic exemplars who work upon the shape of their sensibilities even as they embrace those creeds.

The question inevitably arises: What, according to this view, do you do about those who militantly refuse the quest to engage the relational dimension of faith in this way? Not much, at first. You do seek to *inspire* in them the importance of this task to the contemporary world, proceeding on one front by identifying elements in their own traditions supportive of such a project and on another by acknowledging publicly the comparative contestability of elements in your own faith. For thinking and judgment are affected by inspiration, attraction, and example as well as by the logic of argument. Better, the former ingredients mix into the latter recipes.

But let's cut to the chase. What about those who take violence against you in the name of their faith? Some will argue, of course, that faith is not a real factor here: the veneer of faith is reducible to something else such as economic need or ambition or the dictates of territorial sovereignty. Such arguments may capture part of the truth some of the time. But they are captured themselves by a prior judgment that religion is never a determining element in itself.

Others, who do play up the importance of religious motives, such as Jesus, Epicurus, Spinoza, and Nietzsche, acknowledge the importance of faith. But in different ways they seek to "pass by" poisonous people who seek to impose their faiths on others. That strategy provides a starting point, but it does not suffice either.[23] Here is a supplement. If the opponents are indeed violent—that is, if they use violence against you when you have not sought to colonize or silence them—it may well be necessary to take military or police action against them to forestall the return of that violence. However, once you acknowledge the potential for evil within every faith, including your own, you will also attend to the insistence by some proponents of your own faith to exaggerate and overgeneralize this danger. You now take another look around at the public representations of alternative faiths by your allies. And you explore how to reengage those who, while not directly making violent attacks against you, provide the attackers with material and spiritual conditions of support. You explore how to reduce the passive tolerance of violence. Here, war is not the answer.

In addressing a fund of passive tolerance in predominantly Muslim countries for terrorism against America, for instance, you attend to the history of aggression and colonization by predominantly Christian states in those areas; you publicly oppose preemptive wars by your own state; you publicly confess the contestability of the faith that inspires you; you engage moderate voices in the other faith; and you push the United States to support aggressively a state of Palestine in the territory now occupied by Israel. In these ways, and others too, you work upon your faith and state to curtail its drive to the negation of alternative faiths.

Identifying admirable beacons within your own faith is pertinent to the inspirational dimension of ethico-political life. Take Bartoleme de las Casas. This Spanish Christian priest traveled with the Conquistadors to the New World in the sixteenth century, armed with the Augustinian version of Christianity and a heartfelt obligation to convert the heathen. But as he saw and felt the horrendous effects of that project upon the Aztecs, the creed of universalism and conversion that he confessed gradually gave ground to the reservoir of Augustinian love infusing his faith. He looked with new eyes at these bearers of an alien faith, revising the self-fulfilling representations of them as purveyors of idolatry, sacrifice, and sodomy which had made it all too easy to vindicate the Spanish-Christian imperative of conquest and conversion. He showed, for example, how their statues were not idols but *symbols* of divinity that corresponded rather well to the Christian relation between the Cross and divinity. This man of faith struggled against the temptation to evil within the Christian-state constellation of his day, expressed through denigrating representations and forced conversions. He did so by drawing sustenance from the Augustinian sensibility of love overflowing the creed in which it was set. Under the stress of participation in violence, his Christian sensibility first disrupted dimensions of his own faith and then became a reserve to draw upon in reworking its relational dimension. Responding creatively to an unexpected twist in time—the discovery of a whole new world of non-Christians—he became an early Christian voice in support of religious pluralism.[24] He took a step beyond both Augustine and Spinoza in that respect.

Most pertinent today are the millions upon millions of people of diverse faiths in numerous regimes who work upon themselves, their faith communities, and their states to curtail the potential for evil inside the inordinate demand for correspondence between faith and territorial sovereignty. They acknowledge the ubiquity of faith to life while perceiving the potential for evil within it. Doing so, they periodically find it incumbent to oppose drives to self-righteous violence by their own religious leaders and by the territorial states that govern them.

CHAPTER 2

PLURALISM AND
RELATIVISM

The Bounds of Pluralism

Straussianism is the only professorial movement in the United States that has attained the standing of a public philosophy. Since at least the late 1970s its proponents have not only played a significant role in the academy, but many have served as presidential advisers when a Republican has held office and as talking heads on Fox News, CNN, and MSNBC when Republicans have been in or out of office. The tendency is to counsel respect for the office of the presidency when a Republican is in office, in the name of civic virtue, and to subject the incumbent to relentless critique when a Democrat holds office. Reagan and the two Bushes have been recipients of the honor; Carter and Clinton recipients of the line of attack. Let's explore the contribution that Leo Strauss himself has made to contemporary Straussian public philosophy, as well as limits that he may set to such a movement.

In *Liberalism, Ancient and Modern*, published in the 1960s, Strauss argues in favor of a classical liberal education and against the shape that modern liberalism has taken. Liberal education, in the classic sense, prepares an élite of gentlemen to lift mass democracy to a higher level of achievement: "Liberal education is the counterpoison to mass culture, to the corroding effects of mass culture, to its inherent tendency to produce nothing but 'specialists without spirit and voluptuaries without heart.' Liberal education is the ladder by which we try to ascend from mass democracy to democracy as originally meant. Liberal education is the necessary endeavor to found an aristocracy within democratic mass society. Liberal education reminds those members of a mass democracy who have ears to hear, of human greatness."[1]

Waiving reservations about his use of the term "mass," I agree that liberal education makes an indispensable contribution to the nobility of democracy. The issue is what type of nobility to foster. What kind of civic virtue is to be nourished? A chapter on "The Liberalism of Classical Political Philosophy" provides insight into Strauss's view. Here Strauss presents a scathing review of a book by Eric Havelock on liberalism in classical Greek political philosophy. Havelock wrote before the philosophy of John Rawls had achieved hegemony among liberal academics in America. Strauss, while rebuking Havelock for "unsurpassed shallowness and crudity" in his reading of Greek classics, also gives us an idea of how the "modern liberalism," of which Havelock is a prototype, looks to him.[2] My purpose is not to defend Havelock's reading of ancient Greek thinkers, but to probe Strauss's account of modern liberalism through his critique of Havelock.

Havelock, he writes, thinks that every value is " 'negotiable' because he is extremely tolerant."[3] Strauss himself wonders whether tolerance can be spread so widely, "whether Tolerance can remain tolerant when confronted with unqualified Intolerance."[4] The modern liberal also asserts, crucially, "that man's being is accidental to the universe,"[5] though he is mistaken if he imagines that most classic Greek thinkers agreed with him. The modern liberal also thinks "that man's nature and therewith morality are essentially changing."[6] Strauss, reasonably enough, objects to Havelock's criticizing Plato for not having set forth the liberalism of his day before submitting it to criticism. "Plato failed to set forth the liberal view," Strauss writes, "because the liberal view did not exist."[7] Plato criticized sophistry, not liberalism. But why did he use myth as well as argument to do so? "We on our part suggest this explanation. Plato knew that most men read more with their 'imagination' than with open-minded care and are therefore much more benefitted by salutary myths than by the naked truth. Precisely the liberals who hold that morality is historical or of merely human origin must go on to say . . . that this invaluable acquisition . . . is 'too precious to be gambled with': the greatest enemies of civilization in civilized countries are those who squander the heritage . . . ; civilization is much less endangered by narrow but loyal preservers than by the shallow and glib futurists, who, being themselves rootless, try to destroy all roots and thus do everything in their power in order to bring back the initial chaos and promiscuity. The first duty of civilized man is then to respect his past."[8]

Again, "There is undoubtedly some kinship between the modern liberal and the ancient sophist. Both are unaware of the existence of a problem of civilization, although to different degrees. For Protagoras supplies his assertions with important qualifications which do not come out in Havelock's paraphrases. The utmost one can say about his whole discussion is that it sheds some light on present day liberalism."[9]

So Strauss, like me, is concerned with a threat to modern civilization. In this context he offers his most grave objection to Havelock, and by implication, modern liberalism: "Through that philosophy the humane desire for tolerance is pushed to the extreme where tolerance becomes perverted into abandonment of all standards and hence of all discipline, including philological discipline. But absolute tolerance is altogether impossible; the allegedly absolute tolerance turns into ferocious hatred of those who have stated most clearly and most forcefully that there are unchangeable standards founded in the nature of man and the nature of things."[10]

I find Strauss's effortless use of such phrases as "enemies of civilization," "squander," "perverted," "shallow and glib futurists," "rootless," "utmost," "abandonment of all standards," and "ferocious hatred" to express a degree of virulence outstripping the intellectual vices of his object of attack. I do, however, agree with him that every political regime must set limits and seek to secure them through education and discipline. For example, a pluralistic society inculcates the virtue of relational modesty between proponents of different faiths and creeds, and it seeks to limit the power of those who would overthrow diversity in the name of religious unitarianism.

Most importantly, pluralism is not the same as cultural relativism, "absolute tolerance," or "the abandonment of all standards," though many of its critics, Straussian and otherwise, treat these perspectives as if they were the same. Cultural relativism is the view that you should support the culture that is dominant in a particular place. The terms "culture" and "place" are key. For relativism is most at home with itself when it is situated in a concentric image of territorial culture. Here culture is said to radiate from the family to larger circles such as neighborhood, locality, and nation. The largest circles of belonging in turn radiate back to the smaller ones, with each circle entering into relations of resonance with the others. Given such an understanding of culture, a relativist is one who supports whatever practices and norms prevail in each concentrically ordered "place." Indeed, it is the concentric image of culture that allows you first to isolate each territorial regime as an enclosed "culture," and then to support the content of each territorial culture so defined. I don't, in fact, know many cultural relativists. For many called relativists by others do not in fact support a concentric image of culture. Rather, absolutists are apt to support such an image of culture, and then to project it back on those they define as relativists.

A pluralist, by comparison, is one who prizes cultural diversity along several dimensions and is ready to join others in militant action, when necessary, to support pluralism against counterdrives to unitarianism. A pluralist is unlikely to define culture through its concentric dimension alone, the definition of culture that allows both relativism and universalism in their simple forms to be. Pluralism, of the sort to be supported here at least, denies the sufficiency of a concentric image of culture to territorial politics. Pluralists are also alert to eccentric connections that cut across the circles of family, neighborhood, and nation, as when ecologists in different parts of the world align to put pressure on several states at once, or gays and their supporters from different families, neighborhoods, communities, and religious faiths press for laws and norms that extend marriage and family, or an alliance of oil magnates from different countries puts pressure on oil-producing states, or a cross-state coalition of citizens presses the United States, Israel, and Palestine to forge a real state in the occupied territory of Palestine. Pluralists are attentive both to established connections that exceed the concentric image of culture and to emergent eccentric flows that surge against the grain of the concentric dimension of being, as when new rights for women are taken through political insurgency, or a new right to doctor-assisted death for terminally ill patients is pressed into being from below the previous threshold of recognized rights, or a cross-country citizen movement is organized to alter state environmental practices. Pluralists do not figure the eccentric as that which is necessarily isolated. Only those who reduce culture to its concentric dimension do that.

Pluralists, given their experience of the complexity of culture, often find themselves pressed to decide which of these parties to support, which to oppose, and which to meet with studied indifference. A pluralist can thus seldom bestow "unqualified tolerance" on any specific place or circle of being, because the image of culture adopted does not divide territorial places into intercoded circles. Pluralists are not relativists in the first instance because our image of culture encourages us to embrace certain things in this particular place, to be indifferent to some, to be wary of others, and to fight militantly against the continuation of yet others.

We are not relativists in a second and a third sense, as well. Pluralists set limits to tolerance to ensure that an exclusionary, unitarian movement does not take over an entire regime—that is, to ensure that a territorial regime does not become too concentric and too closed. Moreover, we also define a set of *general virtues and limits* needed to nourish a pluralist ethos within a territorial regime. Granted, we are cautious in setting *final* limits in advance to the scope of diversity. For we are attuned to the dicey history of how absolute limits posed at one time in Europe or America were revealed later to have fostered grave suffering and to have been unnecessary to effective governance. Take, for starters, ideas heretofore widespread in the West: that the citizens of a regime must be Christian, that only men can be citizens, that only heterosexuals can participate openly in public life, that racial mixing is impermissible miscegenation, that only landed gentlemen are qualified to govern a state, that marriage must be restricted to the relation between men and women, and that avowed atheists are too unreliable to serve as elected public officials. It is thus necessary to set limits, *but pluralists are critical of the self-confidence with which many unitarians endow already existing limits with eternal necessity.*

It is necessary to set limits, partly because it is impossible to house every possible mode of diversity in the same regime at the same time. And it is necessary to organize militantly when pluralism is under grave duress from unitarian movements. You encourage a wide diversity of religious faiths, sensual habits, household organizations, ethnic traditions, gender practices, and so on, and you encourage the civic virtues of pluralism to inform relations between these constituencies. But a democratic pluralist won't willingly, for instance, allow the state to torture prisoners; murder to go unpunished; parents to deprive their children of an education; the public school system to deteriorate; wealthy citizens to evade taxes; orphaned children to be placed under the care of incompetent adults; adult citizens to be unemployed for too long; the gap between the real cost of living in a system and the income-earning ability of most citizens to grow large; the income hierarchy to become too extreme; or narrow unitarians to take charge of the regime. Pluralists thus agree with Strauss that "absolute tolerance is altogether impossible," even as we set some of those limits at different points and places.

Moreover, a diverse culture is one in which pluralistic *virtues* of public accountability, self-discipline, receptive listening, gritted-teeth tolerance of some things you hate, and a commitment to justice are widespread. Pluralism, particularly of the multidimensional, embedded variety supported here, requires a set of civic virtues to support itself. We shall discuss them more closely in later chapters.

But what is the "ground" or "basis" of pluralist virtues? Must they not, at least, come from a single, universal source? And how authoritative and certain is that ground? When Strauss refers to the liberal's "ferocious hatred of those who have stated most clearly and most forcefully that there are unchangeable standards founded in the nature of man and the nature of things," it seems reasonable to assume that he endorses unchangeable standards anchored in a single source. Perhaps he does. But he also says in the first statement quoted earlier, "Plato knew that most men read more with their 'imagination' than with open-minded care and are therefore much more benefitted by salutary myths than by the naked truth." And a couple of times in the same book Strauss writes that he sometimes inserts his own beliefs into the words of others rather than stating them directly. So it is at least possible that while Strauss thinks the untutored must be made to believe that there is an eternal, undeniable basis of fixed virtue, he himself doubts that the source needed can be demonstrated. If so, one way to protect this politically necessary but philosophically unanchored idea would be to attack vociferously those who publicly call the weight of the anchor into question. The virulence of Strauss's attack on Havelock might express a desire to identify the single, universal basis of virtue *or* Strauss's desire to veil his own skepticism about the ability to provide the ground that civilization needs. It is hard to tell.

Let's pursue this question a step further, turning to an essay in which Strauss engages a great thinker of the past, an essay therefore less freighted with the political passions of Strauss's day. In the "Preface to Spinoza's Critique of Religion," Strauss explores the relation between reason and religious tradition in Spinoza's philosophy. Spinoza is pivotal because he, more than any other figure, launched the modern idea that reason is sufficient to itself, that it need not invoke a contestable element of faith to support itself. After a rich review of responses by Jewish intellectuals in Weimar Germany to Spinoza's thought, Strauss turns to the fundamental issue dividing Jewish orthodoxy from Spinoza's heterodox philosophy. With respect to the orthodox faith in "an omnipotent God whose will is unfathomable, whose ways are not our ways, who has decided to dwell in the thick darkness," Strauss writes, "The orthodox premise cannot be refuted by experience nor by recourse to the principle of contradiction. An indirect proof of this is the fact that Spinoza and his like owed such success as they had in their fight against orthodoxy to laughter and mockery . . . One is tempted to say that mockery does not succeed the refutation of the orthodox tenets, but is itself the refutation."[11]

Indeed, we can now see that Strauss himself inverts Spinoza's strategy, replacing Spinoza's mockery of a personal God with his own invective against the nontheism of Havelock. Mockery weakens orthodox faith, Strauss writes, when it taps into dissonance between the expressed belief of the faithful and other tacit judgments that they make in daily life. If you already doubt at some level that every word in the Pentateuch was asserted by the divinely inspired Moses, Spinoza's presentation of textual evidence that Moses died before the books were finished might threaten your faith. But if your faith in divine inspiration runs deep, or if you think that the masses must accept this faith even if you do not, evidence of the untimely death of Moses merely adds a minor complication to be met in a variety of creative ways. So Spinozist mockery takes a toll on some believers, but Spinozist reason and argument, Strauss asserts, is incapable of providing a definitive refutation of orthodox faith.

> The genuine refutation of orthodoxy would require the proof that the world and human life are perfectly intelligible without the assumption of a mysterious God . . . Spinoza's *Ethics* attempts to be that system but it does not succeed; the clear and distinct account of everything which it presents remains fundamentally hypothetical. As a consequence its cognitive status is not different from that of the orthodox account. Certain it is that Spinoza cannot legitimately deny the possibility of revelation. But to grant that revelation is possible means to grant that the philosophic account and the philosophic way of life are not necessarily, not evidently, the true account and the right way of life; philosophy, the quest for evident and necessary knowledge, rests itself on an unevident decision, on an act of will, just as faith. Hence the antagonism between Spinoza and Judaism, between belief and unbelief, is ultimately not theoretical, but moral.[12]

This is a superb formulation. I endorse much in it. As a neo-Spinozist of sorts myself I concur, for instance, that Spinoza did not succeed in demonstrating the truth of his philosophy of Substance as univocal, or that parallelism of mind and body is true, or that an ethic of cultivation is superior to the morality of law. It is a highly contestable philosophy, one in which those who already have faith in it will find arguments on its behalf more convincing than they otherwise might.

Moreover, no secularist or rationalist since Spinoza has demonstrated the sufficiency of reason to itself either. Orthodox faith in a created world is not apt to be eliminated by argument and laboratory results alone, though recourse to this piece of evidence or that argument might press some of the faithful to clarify their thinking in a new way or to sharpen it through alteration. Many modern Christians and Jews, for instance, have modified elements in their received faiths to render them compatible with evolutionary theory, treating, for instance, Biblical statements that appear to contravene that theory as allegorical.

Faith is sustained by a mixture of cultural devices, including induction at a young age, common rituals, shared stories, urgent calls to loyalty, mockery of other faiths, epiphanic experiences, and public arguments all mixing into each other. Occasionally an argument, unexpected event, expression of mockery, or startling piece of evidence hits a person of this or that faith in just the right way at a vulnerable moment, setting into motion a process that leads eventually to conversion from one faith to another. Surely, for instance, Spinoza's traumatic excommunication as a youth by Jewish Elders in Amsterdam played a role in his later doctrine of how affect and thought are intertwined. Argument alone seldom *suffices* to lodge or dislodge faith. Better, it is hard to see what "argument alone" would look like, since it is interwoven with affect and does its work in conjunction with a series of images, feelings, memories, and desires that it touches.

I also embrace, as indicated in chapter 1, a variant of the Straussian contention that the "antagonism . . . between Spinoza and Judaism, between belief and unbelief, is ultimately not theoretical, but moral." To bring out the points of contact and difference let me expand the formulation a little. The dispute (which does not always have to take the form of an "antagonism") is not exactly between "belief and unbelief," with the implication that one side is filled with belief and the other has a vacancy where belief might have been. It is better articulated as the difference between a positive belief in *transcendence over the world* and a positive belief in the *immanence of the world*. Those inspired by, say, Moses, Paul, Augustine, or Mohammed hold that the world is created, that (in some cases) eternal life is possible, that the human obligation to morality is founded on a divine command in the last instance, and that divine revelation is fundamental to cultivation of religious truth. Others inspired by the likes of Buddha (on some readings), Epicurus, Lucretius, Spinoza, Hume, Nietzsche, and Havelock, on the other hand, confess faith that the world is eternal rather than created, that it is a world of becoming without an intrinsic purpose, and that goodness and nobility are anchored in the first instance in a nonjuridical source such as human love of the complexity of world or the abundance of life, over and above induction into a specific identity. The debate between these two generic faiths has not to date been resolved, despite what some parties on both sides say. The adversaries are inspired in part by contrasting moral judgments, with one set asserting that the world will fall apart unless most people profess belief in transcendence and the other asserting that violent struggles between advocates of different visions of transcendence have brought a load of otherwise unnecessary agony into the world. Strauss himself may believe in a created world; or he may believe that the masses require such a belief even if he does not; or he may support a classic conception of reason as sufficient to itself.[13] I will not try to decide this question.

My view, to put it briefly, is that the most noble response is to seek to transmute cultural antagonisms between transcendence and immanence into debates marked by agonistic respect between the partisans, with each set acknowledging that its highest and most entrenched faith is legitimately contestable by the others. It may be, as "pessimists" eagerly retort, that many believers will refuse such an invitation. But if the cultural *need* for such an ethos is high, if much violence within and between states is traceable to the tenacity of these differences, and if the late modern time is one in which most territorial regimes find themselves populated by partisans of different faiths, creeds, and philosophies, then public intellectuals should lead the way in setting the example, rather than decrying the refusal of others to follow one that they have not yet instantiated sufficiently in their own practices. The pursuit of such an ethos is grounded in the assumption that residing *between* a fundamental image of the world as either created or uncreated and a specific ethico-political stance resides a *sensibility* that colors how that creed is expressed and portrayed to others. The sensibility mixes into the creed, rotating its ethico-political compass in this way or that. An existential faith thus consists of a creed or philosophy plus the sensibility infused into it.

The most urgent need today is to mix presumptively generous sensibilities into a variety of theistic and nontheistic creeds, sensibilities attuned to the contemporary need to transfigure relations of antagonism between faiths into relations of agonistic respect. The idea is not to rise either to one ecumenical faith or to a practice of reason located entirely above faith, but to forge a positive ethos of public engagement between alternative faiths. Of course the difficulties are great and the probabilities may even point in other directions. But the contemporary need is great. Those who invoke pessimism to refuse the pursuit do not take sufficient measure of the contemporary need.

Such a pluralism of creeds, again, does not devolve into relativism. Pluralists think it is extremely important, for instance, *how* people of diverse faiths hold and express their faiths in public space. And we seek to limit the power of those who would invest their own creed with unquestioned territorial hegemony. We think that in a world marked by the coexistence of multiple faiths on most politically organized territories, the horizontal relations between faiths require as much attention as the vertical dimension of each. *Expansive pluralism supports the dissemination of general virtues across diverse faiths.* The key, again, is the relational sensibility with which individuals and communities express their faiths and the general ethos through which relations between alternative faiths are negotiated.

To the extent that Strauss seeks to realize a regime in which one creed rules over others, he folds an exclusionary sensibility into his faith. The exclusionary imperative is an effect less of the creed he embraces and more of the type of sensibility that characterizes it. To the extent that he seeks to realize a world in which multiple faiths interact productively on the same terrain, that too is influenced by the kind of sensibility infused into his faith. The same goes for me. My faith in immanence in the last instance might be joined to a presumptively generous sensibility or to an exclusionary, imperious sensibility.

But why do I, a confessed believer in immanence and supporter of deep pluralism, join Strauss in drawing attention to the power of faith? Why do so, in particular, during a time when so many brim over with faith and many of the faithful in several traditions vindicate violence to nationalize the states they inhabit? Here I follow William James, to whom the same question was posed. James writes, "I quite agree that what mankind at large most lacks is criticism and caution, not faith."[14] Among many, it is the relational sensibility attached to the faith that needs work, not the admission that faith plays an important role. But, James also asserts, he writes in the first instance to other philosophers, most of whom profess either to rise above faith or, more often, to bracket faith when they participate in the domains of science, morality, literary theory, philosophy, social theory, and public life.

James, like me, is dubious about these latter claims. While many express their faith with less relational modesty than needed, the intellectual class tends to repress the role that faith plays in the intellectual enterprise itself. When you press the ubiquity of faith upon the second group, you see that faith need not always be everything or nothing. There is a lot of room between denying faith a constitutive role in life and making it everything. When you see how faith commitments vary in intensity, content, and imperiousness, you set the stage to explore what it takes to engender modesty in the public relations between faiths coexisting on the same territory. And if you include yourself and your faith in the equation, rather than pretending to float above the fray, you place yourself in a better position to commend a pluralist ethos to others.

Americanism and Terrorism

Let's fast-forward from the era of Strauss to today. The prominent neoconservatives William Kristol, William Bennett, and Paul Wolfowitz, the deputy secretary of defense who orchestrated the Iraq invasion during the presidency of George W. Bush, join many other academics and publicists in professing intellectual debts to Leo Strauss. I focus on Bennett, who until recently served as one of the most visible media spokespersons for Reagan-Bush-Bush Republicanism. Between Leo Strauss of the 1950s and 1960s and William Bennett of the onset of the twenty-first century, a

host of events has occurred. There have been new movements in de-
colonization, civil rights, feminism, gay and lesbian rights, sexual liberation, and ecology. On the register of dramatic events there has been the
Vietnam war, the intensification of the Palestinian-Israeli conflict, the
rise of a global, corporate plutocracy, the collapse of the Soviet Union,
the emergence of a conservative majority on the U.S. Supreme Court, the
intensification of a large evangelical Christian movement, the near take-
over of the electronic news media in the United States by the moderate
and bellicose Right, the rapid rise of neoconservative think tanks, 9/11,
the war against Al Qaeda in Afghanistan, the Guantánamo gulag, and the
invasion and occupation of Iraq by an American-led coalition of the
willing.

William Bennett is no Leo Strauss. Is he, though, one of the "gentlemen" whom Strauss says philosophers need to help inject virtue into the
currency of public life? There is in one respect a clear line of descent
from Strauss's philosophical politics, propagated through readings of
classic philosophers, to William Bennett's political admonitions, delivered in popular books, public speeches, and TV interviews. For Bennett
also sees relativism, self-indulgence, and rootlessness all around him,
particularly among those who support multidimensional pluralism. He
finds organized religion, particularly evangelical Christianity, to provide
an essential source of value to America and western civilization. And he
focuses on weaknesses in American education, attacking in strong terms
the "secularism" and "anti-Americanism" of the "professoriate."

Bennett, like Strauss, looks back to a time when values were solid
and the middle class had self-confidence. His descriptions of decadence
resonate with those Strauss gave of the 1950s and 1960s in America.
Unlike Strauss, however, he does not measure modernity against the
ancient Greek world. Rather, he measures the present against the 1950s
in America, the period in which Strauss himself saw classical virtues
succumbing to the rootlessness and relativism of modern liberalism.
When you read Bennett alongside Strauss, seeing the same terms applied to different eras, you discern how efficacious the relentless use of
that rhetoric can be by those hell-bent on occupying the authoritative
center around which diverse minorities are expected to revolve.

Bennett, unlike Strauss, is not wary of the electronic news media.

He lives on and for them. This gentleman, who loves to gamble, would bet a large sum against my wager on the positive relation between pursuing an expansive ethos of multidimensional pluralism and the survival of democratic civilization. I think, as we shall see in chapter 5, that in the age of the suicide bomber it has become even more important to mobilize a cross-state citizen movement to press Israel and the United States to support either a new state of Palestine or a greater Israel with equal citizenship for all residents. Such a direction is not only just to the occupied residents of Palestine, it is also important to the future of democracy in the United States and Europe. In *Why We Fight*, written shortly after the trauma of 9/11, Bennett pursues a different direction. He explains why it is necessary to wage aggressive cultural and military war against the evils of Islam. The American reaction to the trauma of 9/11 has filled him with hope. For he discerns a new unity of purpose in America.

The war on terrorism, he writes, is above all a religious war. In that war America must be wary of the liberal distinction between moderate and extreme Muslims, in either the Middle East or the United States. The first attack against America in 1993 "should have brought home the folly of the then fashionable distinction between 'moderate' and 'extreme' Muslim militants and the absolute need to 'err on the side of caution' in protecting the safety of our citizens."[15] I am not at all confident that Strauss would join Bennett in adopting such an unnuanced position with respect to Muslims.

Bennett, like Strauss, has been critical of secularism in the West because it does not give enough importance to religious faith in supporting essential republican virtues. He would be pleased to know that at least 58 percent of Americans say that you cannot be moral unless you believe in God, while the figure is only around 13 percent in France.[16] He would also be pleased to learn that 81 percent of Americans believe in hell, though it might trouble him that less than 1 percent think they themselves are going to hell. Given Bennett's previous focus on the indispensability of religion to public life it is fascinating to see how he now thinks the Islamic world needs to undergo "the equivalent of the eighteenth-century Enlightenment,"[17] though he is hardly confident it will do so.

Here I am closer to Strauss along one dimension and critical of both him and Bennett along another. I think, first, that exclusionary variants of Judaism, Christianity, Islam, and atheism could all profit from going through the Enlightenment and, second, that the western secularism emerging from the Enlightenment is today too unalert to the role that enactment, discipline, and ritual play in its own mode of being and too self-confident in projecting a clean separation between reason and faith. We need to pass through the Enlightenment, in its dominant modes, coming out at a place that respects its opposition to theocratic governance while simultaneously moving beyond the overbearing confidence in reason that the two dominant wings within it pursued.[18] As you call upon Muslims in Europe and America to be receptive to coexistence with other faiths within the same territory and across territorial divisions, it is indispensable to work upon your own theistic or nontheistic faith to come to terms affirmatively with its relational dimension and the legitimacy of its deep contestability in the hearts and minds of others.

Bennett also believes that both "we" and "they" need to rethink things, but he means that we need to affirm our superiority more confidently while they need to admit our superiority more humbly. When we identify the sources of attacks on us, "Too often we have tacitly accepted a share of that blame, tacitly behaved as if we needed to ask forgiveness for the weakness and backwardness, the corruption and evil, that others have brought on themselves and for which they are solely responsible. If the Islamic world is ever to experience the uplift it has demanded, all this will have to change—on both sides. They will have to cease rejecting Western civilization and instead begin to study it; we will have to cease indulging ourselves in guilt and instead, as the writer Shelby Steele has finely put it, 'allow the greatness of western civilization to speak for itself.' "[19]

According to Bennett, Arabs should study the greatness of western civilization not, however, as it today unveils itself in film, TV dramas, novels, pop music, the professoriate, many Protestant Christian churches, and liberal politicians. Its greatness stands against such relativistic and rootless forces. "Western civilization" functions in Bennett's hands as a weapon to wield against traditions outside it *and* against many of the things that now constitute it. He wages cultural war within "the West" and cultural and military campaigns against Islam outside it.

Bennett does sing the praises of Islam in the late Middle Ages. But I can find no moment where a crack opens to encourage him to listen with new ears to faiths different from those already on his official register of honored faiths. Cultural pluralism to him is not something you draw upon to open yourself a bit, even as you encourage its practice in others. It is a weapon you wield against places and faiths that do not conform to the fixed range of diversity you now accept.

I believe that American-Israeli policy in the Middle East rests too much upon a politics of humiliation against Palestinians, and that such a policy pursued over a long period pushes many residents in Palestine and other predominately Islamic states toward tolerance or passive support of acts of terrorism against Israel, the United States, and assorted European countries. It is essential to hunt down the leaders of Al Qaeda. But that hunt must be joined to concerted efforts to end the Israeli occupation of Palestine, to give Palestine as much financial support as the United States appropriately gives to Israel now, and to inform Israeli settlers on the Palestinian territory that they can either return to Israel or join the new state of Palestine. As we shall see in chapter 5, it is unlikely that elected officials in the United States or Israel will by themselves pursue such a strategy militantly. The dynamics of electoral politics press against it. The momentum to shift priority must be provided by a militant cross-country movement of citizens who press these states from inside and outside simultaneously to initiate the needed action. There is much more to say about this issue. But here I focus on the effect that existing policies have on the future prospects for democratic pluralism within Euro-American states.

The neoconservative policies of invasion and occupation, combined with efforts to tighten borders and security arrangements at home, threaten the internal survival of a robust pluralist democracy. They threaten to turn pluralist democracies against themselves, fostering more closed surveillance states. New patterns of surveillance can easily be installed. But every time you make progress on one front without addressing Muslim grievances abroad and those of Muslim faith on your own territory, new holes, cracks, border porosities, and potential targets automatically emerge elsewhere. If the border between the United States and Mexico is secured, that between the United States and Canada becomes more porous; if air travel is tightened, the food supply system, trains, schools, the computer network, and urban targets of dirty bombs become vulnerable. Airport surveillance, internet filters, passport tracking devices, legal detention without criminal charges, security internment camps, secret trials, "free speech zones," DNA profiles, border walls and fences, erosion of the line between internal security and external military action, and translation of the electronic news media into embedded conduits of mass mobilization—these security activities resonate together, engendering a national security machine that pushes numerous issues outside the range of legitimate dissent and mobilizes the populace to support new security and surveillance practices against underspecified enemies.

William Bennett is a polemicist who mobilizes exclusionary elements within the American state against Muslims at home and predominantly Islamic states abroad. He has lost touch with subtle elements in the thought of the master who inspires him, even while he applies the master's rhetoric of relativism, rootlessness, self-indulgence, misguided tolerance, and superficiality against democrats, liberals, and pluralists in his own state.

In what follows I focus on changes in Euro-American orientations toward Muslims at home that might foster pluralism within these states and better relations abroad. The question of citizen action across states is pursued in chapter 5.

A Special Minority

Strauss is insightful about the predicament of Jews in Europe before the Second World War. He sees that pre-war, secular responses to Judaism promoted legal equality without becoming embedded deeply in public culture. Judgments about who belongs and does not belong are not inscribed in law alone. They also reside in the daily practices of the majority, in how it responds in public places, in the workplace, on stage, in commercial life, at dinner parties, in the courtroom, at the police station, and so on. Strauss quotes Herzl, who said, "We are a nation—the enemy makes us a nation whether we like it or not."[20] The enemy defined Jews as a nonterritorial nation within a territorial state, guaranteeing in so doing that Jews would be treated as a special minority unlike other minorities. Strauss does not think that early Zionism was capable of resolving "the Jewish problem" either.

It is not clear to me how Strauss would extrapolate from these insights today. But the condition of the Jew in European society before the Second World War parallels in one respect the condition of Muslims in Europe and the United States today. There are differences. The Muslim minority here and now, unlike the Jewish minority there and then, has another region to refer or retreat to, where its faith is in charge. And no Jewish faction organizes terrorist attacks against the United States or Europe. The underlying similarity, however, is that many Europeans and Americans today define Muslims as a special minority, as the minority among others that constitutes a nation within a nation, as the minority with distinctive rituals residing outside the orbit of the Enlightenment distinction between private faith and public reason.

It is partly because many who identify with Islamic traditions draw a close connection between their public lives and their faiths that they are said to be unique. We have seen that William Bennett calls for a greater distinction between the public and the private in the Muslim world, even while he supports a reduction of that distance in predominantly Christian America. An insight may be concealed in this double standard.

For there is another way to go on the issue, one reducible neither to the double standard of Bennett, nor to the inculcation of Muslims into the secular division between public faith and private citizenship, nor to the special minoritization of one minority, nor to a theocratic state. Talal Asad, an anthropologist of Islamic heritage who studies the religious practices of both Christians and Muslims, points toward the alternative. He concurs that there is a moment of similarity between Jews of yesteryear and Muslims in Europe and America today. He explores an obscure dimension of contemporary European secularism that unconsciously contributes to this politics of double minoritization.

Consider his critique of Wilfred Cantrell Smith, a Canadian professor of religious studies writing in the 1960s who first sought to distill the essence of "religion" from several world cultures and then drew upon that distillation to compare Islam, Christianity, and Judaism. Smith, Asad writes, thinks of a religious tradition "as a cognitive framework, not as a practical mode of living, not as techniques for teaching body and mind to cultivate specific virtues and abilities that have been authorized, passed on, and reformulated down the generations."[21] As Smith detaches a putative universal to be called "religion" from diverse materializations of culture, he also obscures the operation of such materialities in the religious life of Europe. And he treats the palpable operation of ritual in some variants of Islam as a sign of its underdeveloped character. These two tendencies flow from the way his secular, Protestant reading of religion in general obscures an important component of culture—*its embodiment in repetitive practices that help to constitute the dispositions, sensibilities, and ethos through which meaning is lived, intellectual beliefs are settled, and relations between constituencies are negotiated.* Smith's very distillation of "religion" and "faith" from the materialities of culture situates them within a secular image of a world divided between private rituals and publicly articulated beliefs. It presupposes belief to be neatly separable from ritual practice. This unconscious generalization of the self-image of religious belief within some versions of Protestantism then sets the standard he uses to measure one "religion" against others.

The political upshot of Smith's interpretation becomes visible in Asad's book, *Formations of the Secular*. Here Asad traces how the dominant European idea of religion today expresses a larger cultural unconscious discernible in Smith's work. He contrasts this abstract self-understanding to devotional practices of Christianity in the European Middle Ages; then when the Christian "devotee heard God speak there was a sensuous connection between the inside and outside, a fusion between signifier and signified. The proper reading of scripture . . . depended on disciplining the senses (especially hearing, speech, and sight)."[22] This inner connection between devotional practice and education of the senses gets obscured in many secular, Protestant representations of religion in general: "where faith [within Europe] had once been a virtue, it now acquired an epistemological sense. Faith became a way of knowing supernatural objects, parallel to the knowledge of nature (the *real* world) that reason and observation provided."[23] Now rituals and exercises are understood only to *symbolize* a belief or faith already there, not to participate in the very constitution of faith itself. You can hear echoes of Strauss's account of the ubiquity of faith in Asad's genealogy, even as the sensibility of the two theorists—that is, their sensory orientations and sensual dispositions to diversity—differ.

Of course, if Asad is right the body-brain-culture resonance machine in which we participate continues to flow back and forth between human enactment, institutional discipline, the organization of embedded experience, and the constitution of belief. But many secularists, ministers, theologians, anthropologists, philosophers, and social scientists place such practices within a cognitive framework that either ignores the embedded character of embodied faith, diminishes its importance, or reduces it to modes of cultural manipulation to be transcended by cognitively pure belief. Many cultural theorists speak of the body. But many who do so continue to reduce ritual to a mechanism through which beliefs are *represented* rather than construing it also to be a medium through which embodied habits, dispositions, sensibilities, and capacities of performance are *composed and consolidated*. Atheists too participate in this tendency, when they act as if the only question is whether you "believe" in a transcendent God, accepting in doing so the assumption that cognitive belief or disbelief is both the one critical element and something distinct from education of the senses. "The idea that there is a single clear 'logic of atheism' is itself the product of a modern binary—belief or unbelief in a supernatural being."[24]

Under these conditions Euro-American Protestants and secularists are apt to obscure those shared practices of dress, demeanor, perception, gesture, and meditation that help to compose *their* orientations to being, even as they focus on them in a relatively unfamiliar constituency. They are apt, that is, to reduce the self-understanding of their own faith to a set of abstract *beliefs* while concluding that a Muslim minority lacks the secular division between private belief and public behavior marking a tolerant society.

Many contemporary Euro-American secularists—both the majority who privately profess belief in a transcendent God and the minority who do not—fasten onto this issue, contending that the problem of "Islamic faith" inside and outside Europe is generated by the failure of its adherents to accept the division between freedom of private faith and participation in democratic governance of the state by citizens who bracket their faith when entering the public fray. Both nationalists on the Right and secular liberals contend that "the de-essentialization of Islam is paradigmatic for all thinking about the assimilation of non-European peoples to European civilization."[25] The critical point is that if and as you discern how faith and demeanor are connected you also become less confident about the secular picture of a wall between private faith and public reason.

Asad does not claim that Muslims in Europe make no contribution to the difficulties they face. They do. Those who constitute their faith as the one true, universal faith properly governing others on the same territory can experience themselves to be persecuted merely because the political regime in which they participate does not elevate their faith into the governing faith. In that respect they mirror the demands of that cadre of Jews, Christians, and atheists who demand territorial hegemony for their faiths. Asad suggests, however, that the negotiation of a new pluralism in Europe will *also* involve reassessment on the part of secular, enlightened Europeans of their own tendency to treat belief as neatly separable from disciplinary practices, cultural routines, and the education of sensory experience. Augustine knew these things too. He knew, for instance, that confession voiced in the right way in the proper mood of devotion helps to embed the faith it articulates. Even Kant discerned a connection between "gymnastics" and belief.

Indeed, the most popular definition of contemporary "Europe" itself—as presented by those constituencies who define themselves to embody its essence—is that to be European is to express religious belief in the private realm and to participate as abstract citizens in the public. This innocent and tolerant-sounding definition quietly elevates modern

Christians into the center of Europe and shuffles many Muslims into a minority unlike other minorities. The latter are now said to be distinctive because they alone are unwilling or unable to abide by the modern agenda.

One might add that for secular believers religion is safely relegated to the private realm only because secularists also contend that there is an independent way of reaching authoritative public agreements without recourse to the diverse religious faiths of citizens. The problem is that different secular sects nominate different instruments to fill this role; and each instrument diverges significantly from the others on what that authoritative practice is or could be. Some place their faith in the dictates of public reason, others in deliberative consensus, others in transparent procedures, others in implicit contractual agreements, and still others in a "myth" of equality that citizens accept *as if* it were ontologically grounded. This failure to agree on the authoritative mode of public discourse expresses below the threshold of secular attention the persistent connection between belief, embodiment, and practice. None of these images of public life folds the operational reflexivity needed *into* faith practices themselves. They do not, in my view, because they pretend to identify *a forum entirely above faith through which to regulate diverse faiths.* If the nobility of secularism resides in its quest to enable multiple faiths to coexist on the same public space, its shallowness resides in the hubris of its distinction between private faith and public reason.

Embedded Faith and Deep Pluralism

If Asad's analysis clarifies an element in the double minoritization of Muslims in Europe and America, it also speaks to many orthodox Catholics, Jews, evangelical Protestants, and obdurate atheists. Taken together, these minorities may make up a majority of minorities in several countries.[26] Many of them feel that the privatization of religion and the corollary reduction of faith to a pile of epistemic beliefs has minoritized them in a double way too, if perhaps not as radically. So the issue posed with reference to Muslims in Europe is important to Muslims, to adherents of other faith practices, and to the larger question of how to forge a robust pluralist ethos of engagement out of multiple minorities of religious being.

What, from the point of view of secularism, does it take to "de-essentialize" faith? For John Rawls, for instance, it seems to involve three things: first, to subtract from each practice of faith the demand that it provide the authoritative center around which state politics rotates; second, to disconnect belief (but not its symbolic expression) from devout enactments and ritual performances; third, to reach consensus on a discourse of public justice that rises above the diversity of private faiths while being compatible with most.[27] The doctrine of embedded pluralism that I embrace concurs with Rawlsian secularism in asking advocates of each faith practice, including Christianity, to give up the first demand, because this is the minimal concession that each must make to foster common governance on the same strip of territory without significant violence or oppression. My perspective breaks, however, with classical secularism on the second expectation. For that expectation, as already suggested, rests upon a superficial reading of the complex relation between devotional mood, performance, and belief. Once you modify the understanding of the second condition, it becomes pertinent to reconstitute the third expectation as well. To put the point briefly, you transfigure the drive to reach a consensus on justice above contending faiths into the effort to negotiate a positive ethos of engagement between multiple constituencies who bring chunks and pieces of their faiths with them into the public realm.

It is pertinent to see how the Rawlsian image of secularism also coalesces with the image of state relations assumed in realist and neorealist international relations theory. According to these accounts the Westphalian accord in early modern Europe recognized the sovereignty of each European state over its citizens by pushing religious differences into the private realm. So domestic liberal theory and international relations theory in the West converge upon the assumption of privatized religion. But again, if Asad is correct Christendom has never been privatized in Euro-American states to the degree that proponents of secularism and the Westphalian accord assume. To pursue a new pluralism appropriate to the contemporary world is therefore to come to terms with the expansion of religious diversity inside western states, the critical role that practice plays in constituting religious life as well as in representing it, the effects that the acceleration of pace and interdependence have had on citizen movements to foster multidimensional diversity within and across states, and the effects that all these process have had on the double minoritization of many Muslims within Euro-American states.

Here we focus on what it takes to pluralize faith within Europe and the United States, reserving related issues for later chapters. Three inter-coded ingredients are critical: multidimensional pluralization, positive cultivation of the element of dissonance or mystery within a faith, and secondary practices of relational modesty added to devotional rituals.

First is the need to extend the *dimensions* or *types* of legitimate di-versity within the state. In a culture of multidimensional pluralism you do not simply honor diverse faiths and ethnic practices, you also ex-tend diversity into gender practices, marriage arrangements, linguistic use, sensual affiliations, and household organization. As these multiple kinds of diversity become embedded in corporations, schools, the mili-tary, and the composition of elected officials, *numerous constituencies now acquire more leverage to press their faith communities from within to honor that variety.* The cumulative effect is a healthy politics of creedal ventila-tion within each faith as well as between faiths.[28] Such creedal ventilation uncovers an elasticity of language and governance already simmering in each institutional creed, particularly when each is considered across a long stretch of time. The new social movements within faith commu-nities make this element of elasticity more transparent to the faithful by contracting the time it takes to manifest itself.

More importantly yet, together such movements disperse the mythic assumption through which conservative defenders of the religiously cen-tered nation portray the collective life. Such movements disperse the appearance of a national center occupied by one constituency that affirms the same faith, uses the same language, displays the same skin color, con-forms to the same marriage practices, and participates in the same sen-sual affiliations. The national image of a centered majority surrounded by minorities eventually becomes transfigured into an image of inter-dependent minorities of different types connected through multiple lines of affiliation. This effect is accomplished both by bringing multiple minorities out of the closet and by amplifying public awareness of a multidimensional diversity that is already in motion below the static images through which defenders of the national center represent the world. The most positive result of such a process is to transfigure the myth of a centered majority that tolerates or represses a set of discrete minorities ranged around it into a visible culture of interdependent minorities of multiple types negotiating a generous ethos of governance between them. In the most promising scenario each individual and every constituency now becomes a minority along one or more dimensions.[29]

As we shall see, no automatism governs this process; it can be derailed at any point. It is almost as susceptible to derailment as the pursuit of the unified nation is to the violent repression of selected minorities or devolution into cultural or civil war between militant contenders seeking to occupy the authoritative center.

Second, when the politics of multidimensional minoritization is well under way it may *amplify* within each institutional faith an experience already there. For, as we already suggested in chapter 1, most institutional faiths are punctuated by a moment of mystery, abyss, rupture, openness, or difference within the faith that complicates or confounds the experience of faith. It is precisely at this point in its own practices that the faithful identify a stutter in their own creed, sometimes drawing upon this sense of creedal insufficiency to inspire presumptive generosity toward other creeds. For Christians this might be the element of mystery emphasized by Augustine or of trembling emphasized by Kierkegaard; for Buddhists it might be the point at which the apparently solid self encounters the absence of the ego in a world without a designing God; for Muslims it might be that moment of mystical reception of the difference between finitude and infinity; for nontheists it might be the element of abundance, creativity, and unpredictability that inhabits a world of becoming; and for Jews it might be the ineffable dimension of divinity that makes it inappropriate to name the Nameless one. In each case the gap opens up an element of mystery, rupture, or difference that evades or resists definitive interpretation.

This internal element, indeed, is fateful for the politics of pluralism. For it is at this juncture that some of the faithful are moved either to deny such a moment in the interests of asserting political hegemony over other faiths or, ironically, to claim that other faiths entirely lack such a sense, making the others appear more dogmatic than they are. It is the moment when, in effect, many are tempted to call devotees of other faiths either faithless, relativist, and rootless or dogmatic, legalistic, and closed, doing either or both to vindicate their marginalization or worse. There is a long history of this, of course. We enumerated one fateful example in the last chapter in our brief encounter with Las Casas. Sometimes it acquires an ironic twist, as when Kantian Christians asserted that Jewish legalism made its proponents unalert to the rupture in faith and therefore unqualified to be full citizens in Europe. Today, I call attention to a variant of this phenomenon that may still fall below the radar of some defenders of the religions of the Book. For they sometimes assert with confidence that faith in *transcendence*—which might assume the shape of Christ, Allah, the Nameless one, or a more faint whisper yet—draws you to the experience of a rupture or domain of mystery in faith; but faith in *immanence*—in a world of becoming without a divine force above it—projects overweening confidence that the world is without rupture, or knowable in the last instance, or subject to consummate human control. At this point I only suggest that such a reading misrepresents several philosophies of immanence by failing to appreciate the doctrine of time out of joint in which they are set. The issue will be pursued in chapter 4. Such misrepresentations can have fateful consequences, as the long, ugly history of Euro-American orientations to atheism testifies.

Assuming, then, that most faiths encounter a disruptive moment within the faith, the response of participants to this internal rupture can be fateful to the possibility of pluralism. The response might foster pluralism or marshal its repression. There is, in my judgment, no definitive causal process or undeniable moral law that governs the outcome. It depends above all, as our earlier foray into Straussian theory indicated, upon the sensibilities that the faithful cultivate, the decisions they make, and the ethos they seek to negotiate. That's why, at this point and others too, pluralism emerges as a possibility to pursue rather than the certain effect of determinate conditions. To the extent that it is attained, it remains a fragile achievement to be cherished rather than an outcome to take for granted.[30] The most that can be said is that in an age when multiple minorities of numerous types coexist on the same territory, considerable pressures emerge to amplify the dimension of difference or mystery within each faith. To the extent that pressure is affirmed without resentment rather than repressed or resented, the promise of a positive ethos of engagement between faiths begins to shine. For that same reason some within each faith will resist this process.

In a political culture of deep pluralism with a twist, each faith practices its specific rituals, and each faith minority brings pieces and dimensions of its faith into the public realm with it when the specific issue in question makes it pertinent to do so. Deep pluralism thereby reinstates the link between practice and belief that had been artificially severed by secularism; and it also overturns the impossible counsel to bracket your faith when you participate in politics. But to support the possibility of multiple faiths negotiating with dignity on the same territory, each faith minority also amplifies awareness of the element of rupture or mystery already simmering in it. It responds affirmatively to the preliminary sense of rupture in faith as well as to other ingredients in its faith that counsel generosity to others. This carries us to the third ingredient. For the affirmative relational link in question is cultivated in part by mixing into faith-imbued practices of devotion secondary practices that prepare you to participate with forbearance and presumptive generosity in a larger ethos of pluralism. In the ideal case each faith thereby *embeds* the religious virtue of hospitality and the civic virtue of presumptive generosity into its relational practices. It inserts relational modesty into its ritual practices to amplify one side of its own faith—the injunction to practice hospitality toward other faiths coexisting with it—and to curtail pressures within it to repress or marginalize other faiths.

To participate in the public realm does not now require you to leave your faith at home in the interests of secular reason (or one of its surrogates); it involves mixing into the relational practice of faith itself a preliminary readiness to negotiate with presumptive generosity and forbearance in those numerous situations where recourse to the porous rules of commonality across faiths, public procedure, reason, or deliberation are insufficient to the issue at hand.

But what could attract multiple constituencies to such an agenda?

Negotiation of such an ethos of pluralism, first, honors the embedded character of faith; second, gives expression to a fugitive element of care, hospitality, or love for difference simmering in most faiths; third, secures specific faiths against persecution; and fourth, offers the best opportunity for diverse faiths to coexist without violence while supporting the civic conditions of common governance. It does not issue in a simple universalism in which one image of transcendence sets the standard everywhere or in a cultural relativism in which one faith prevails here and another there. It is neither universalism nor relativism in the simple mode of each.[31] It is deep pluralism. A pluralism that periodically must be defended militantly against this or that drive to religio-state unitarianism.

The public ethos of pluralism pursued here, again, solicits the active cultivation of pluralist virtues by each faith and the negotiation of a positive ethos of engagement between them. Unlike the versions of liberalism and relativism that Strauss and Bennett oppose, I am thereby a proponent of civic virtue. But the public virtues embraced are pluralist virtues. The civic virtues of pluralism, in turn, must become embedded in numerous institutional practices for a positive ethos of pluralism to be.

Such modulating practices are already operative to some degree in many, perhaps most, faith practices. They are also more densely sedimented into other rituals of everyday life than many theological and secular intellectualists admit.[32] They find expression in the multimedia worlds of family ritual, neighborhood gossip, classroom routine, dormitory and urban apartment living, occupational disciplines, professional practices, individual exercises, films, and TV dramas. Such cultural practices mix image, word, rhythm, music, and other nonconceptual sounds to help compose the relational, thought-imbued moods that inhabit us.

Here William Bennett and I concur, though the specific practices I support may be those he mocks or condemns. Bennett, for instance, is unlikely to be impressed with the social relations that emerge from the minutiae of experience in the film *L'Auberge espagnol*. In it, young Europeans from several countries, crowded into one small apartment in Barcelona, find themselves negotiating multiple differences lodged on several layers of being. The sexual appetite of one is balanced against the visceral restraint of others; one guy's attraction to women is viscerally informed by living close to a woman whose trials and joys in a same-sex relationship touch and diverge from his; experimentation with different languages, initiated by the need of each housemate to answer phone calls from relatives, friends, and lovers of the other housemates, exposes limits in one's previous horizons while expanding them modestly; cafe dances, walking the streets, humor, and periodic common meals further link people who are encouraged to modulate their backgrounds and faiths in this way or that. Such a pluralism of everyday collage feeds into the larger politics of public pluralism, showing each participant that one's faith, sexuality, language, cooking habits, and temperament, while pertinent in different degrees and times to the larger life of Europe, do not exhaust everything pertinent to living together across multiple modes of difference. Europe is being recreated through such micro-political, layered practices of connection across multiple differences.

The ennobling of pluralism, to the extent that it occurs, moves back and forth between microscopic negotiation of mundane issues among multiple minorities, reflexive work upon the relational dimension of their own faith practices by specific constituencies, and public engage-ment with larger issues of the day. It is the endless circuits back and forth that do the most productive work.

But still, even after its attractions and collective benefits are enumer-ated, does not participation in deep pluralism require more motivation than that adduced so far? Yes. Each set of participants draws upon a different mix of principles, practices, desires, and incentives to foster the general ethos. Support is grounded partly in care for the late modern condition that multiplies minorities on the same territory, partly in a desire to ensure that you do not become a minority persecuted by others, partly in an interest to protect the survival of democracy under the dis-tinctive conditions of late modern life, partly in recognition of the em-bedded character of your own faith as well as that of others, partly in specific injunctions to love, generosity, charity, or hospitality that help to compose specific faith practices, partly in a desire to avoid participation in otherwise unnecessary modes of violence fomented by calls to na-tional unity, and most of all in a distinctive compound of these motives and habituations that varies in texture from case to case. The hope is that these motives, incentives, interests, and ideals amplify each other, engendering a pluralist resonance machine.

Tolerance of negotiation, mutual adjustment, reciprocal folding in, and relational modesty are, up to a point, cardinal virtues of deep pluralism. The limit point is reached when pluralism itself is threatened by powerful unitarian forces that demand the end of pluralism in the name of defeating "relativism," "nihilism," or "rootlessness." At a certain point of danger—which cannot be specified with precision in advance—a militant assemblage of pluralists, with each party drawing upon modes of inspiration that do not coincide with that of the others, must coalesce to resist such an onslaught. Before that point is reached it is important to identify muted ways by which the contemporary politics of anathematization proceeds. For when intercultural connections are intensive and extensive, the anathematizations of one day readily degenerate into the politics of repression, cleansing, invasion, or liquidation on the next.

Deep pluralism with a bicameral edge foments challenges to cultural relativism, shallow conceptions of secular diversity, and unitarian ideals of politics alike. To the extent that it responds affirmatively to the contemporary acceleration of pace and diversification marking the contemporary age, deep pluralism carries forward through alteration noble elements in the Enlightenment, democracy, and religions of the Book.

CHAPTER 3

PLURALISM AND THE UNIVERSE

A Pluralistic Cosmos

Pluralism in ethico-political life, while controversial, is a relatively clear idea. It involves multidimensional diversity and a bicameral orientation to citizenship. The version endorsed here also addresses the constitutive tension between already existing diversity and the politics of becoming by which new constituencies struggle to modify the register of legitimate diversity.

William James, the American pragmatist and hesitant Protestant, goes further. He claims that the universe itself is pluralistic. He also acknowledges that this very thesis is profoundly contestable. So he is a pluralist in two senses: in the image of the universe that he embraces and in his appreciation that others might legitimately adopt other images of it. He insists that other philosophical faiths about the ultimate character of the universe make a claim upon his respect if not his concurrence. And he strives to make such a bicameral orientation reciprocal. We will examine metaphysical bicameralism as it unfolds in *A Pluralistic Universe*.

James knows roughly what he opposes: (a) that variant of mechanistic materialism which posits a unified world knowable through fixed laws unconnected to any power above nature; (b) monistic rationalism or absolutism, which postulates a rational whole in which we are set, providing us with transcendent obligations to pursue; (c) traditional Christian dualism, which projects an omnipotent, commanding God presiding over both nature and humanity. These metaphysical faiths are susceptible to endless elaboration and clarification. But one kind of objection is said to apply to all of them. All, in one way or another, require us to "apprehend the absolute as if it were a foreign being."[1] The first does so by treating nature as if it were radically different from the human experience of freedom and time. The second does so by treating the everyday experience of disjointedness in the world as if it were illusory and in need of translation into the doctrine of a fully explicable world. The third does so by treating God as an external being radically unlike human beings. This set of objections reveals the link that James maintains between lived experience of the world, the existential hopes and fears that he invests in those experiences, and his fundamental philosophy. He does not think these three elements can be separated neatly. Those who do think such separations can be made are called "intellectualists" by him. An intellectualist either thinks that the shape of categorical distinctions adopted by rationalists can be brought into line with the world is it is, separate from those categories, or that we are compelled by the character of unbreakable subjective necessities to act *as if* this must be so, that is to "postulate" it to be so. An intellectualist also underplays the role that bodily experience and a rich multiplicity of affective states play inside thought, judgment, and action. James resists both versions. He also thinks that the logical empiricism of his day presupposes Kantianism rationalism. It does so by adopting abstract understandings of space, time, and cause within which it seeks to fit all experience.

James, in turn, thinks that human experience exposes some affinities between us and the world, affinities that we can build upon in developing our philosophies and theologies. Materialists, monists, and dualists also participate in this process, but they too often cover up that participation as they present their findings. They are intellectualists.

James in this respect is a partner of Henri Bergson, whose philosophy of time we examine in the next chapter, and a precursor to thinkers such as Wittgenstein, Heidegger, and Merleau-Ponty. All emphasize how we are already engaged with the world before we develop systematic theories, epistemologies, and philosophies about it; all claim that these prior engagements both enable such philosophies to emerge and provide critical resources to turn to in appraising their successes, limits, and failures.

I do not intend to criticize the definitions that James gives of the alternatives he sets himself against, though it is possible to do so. I will treat this part of his essay as a clearing operation, designed to open the space in which the idea of a pluralistic universe is elaborated.

But what is the philosophy of a pluralistic universe? The disturbing, or beguiling, thing is that such a philosophy is not, in James's presentation, susceptible to neat, clean delineation. His view is that the overlapping forces propelling the world are themselves messy. Pluralism is the philosophy of a messy universe. James makes this point in the process of contrasting his position to that of "absolutism," the perspective which contends that we must postulate an "all-form" in which we are set, even if that whole itself is not now susceptible to our full knowledge of it. By comparison, "the pluralistic view which I prefer to adopt is willing to believe that there may ultimately never be an all-form at all, that the substance of reality may never get totally connected, that some of it may remain outside of the largest combination of it ever made, and that a distributive form of reality, the each-form, is logically as acceptable, and empirically as probable as the all-form commonly acquiesced in as so obviously the self-evident thing."[2]

Several vintage Jamesian themes are discernible in this formulation. He speaks of the "view which I prefer to adopt." James thinks that the to and fro of evidence and argument is essential to the development of a philosophy. But he also thinks it unlikely that any specific combination of evidence and argument will suffice to reduce the number of defensible philosophical faiths to one. You would have to be an "intellectualist" to think otherwise after canvassing the variety of philosophies in the history of western and eastern thought, and the variety of credible views that still persist. For the arguments we make have a persistent porosity and uncertainty attached to them. We pour some of our hopes, fears, and anxieties, as they have developed through our respective biographies, into those arguments and conclusions. Philosophy is an art form, not a tight mode of argumentation by which necessary conclusions are drawn.

There is for James an intimate connection between the sensibility of a philosopher and the kind of philosophy adopted. It is not that character determines philosophy, for to say that would be to subtract the pertinence of argument and evidence from it. James never does that. But character does help to *inflect* philosophy. The lived experience of a philosopher enters into the range of philosophical alternatives entertained as plausible or acceptable and the relative weights given to options inside this set. He is impressed by the role that "the will to believe" plays in philosophical commitment. It comes into play as you winnow down the options to those that become viable alternatives. Within that range—a range influenced by contemporary habits of argument, the historical distribution of religious faiths, the contemporary shape of science, and the political affiliations of the day——a philosopher is free to "believe" in the philosophy that speaks to his intimate experience of the world and his hopes for it.

The first thing that makes James a pluralist is therefore his reading of the intimate connection between character, history, and philosophy and his corollary judgment that at any given moment a plurality of philosophies is apt to be placed on the stage of history for articulation and debate. Philosophy itself is pluralistic, in the sense that a plurality of fundamental views can reasonably contend for priority at any single time.

But James is a pluralist in another sense, too. He suggests, again, that "the substance of reality may never get totally collected, that some of it may remain outside of the largest combination of it ever made." This is an opaque formulation, but perhaps no darker than those about the ultimate coherence of the world projected by other philosophies. What does it mean? To me it means a few things:

—That there is no omnipotent, omniscient God outside or above the world who gathers all of the universe together into one system of intelligible relations, though there may be a limited God who participates as one important actor among others in the world.

—That the most refined laws of nature, which scientists have elaborated for complex systems and are apt to elaborate, function as loose approximations or incomplete summaries. This comes out best when you examine the trajectory of the entities in question over a sufficiently long period, a long time for biological evolution, a shorter time for the evolution of human politics. The anomalies, paradoxes, mutations, and gaps in the record encountered by, say, evolutionary biologists can be taken as *signs* of a certain turgidity in the flow of time, within which a measure of uncertainty operates and out of which new things sometimes ferment.

—That if by agent you mean a being or entity that makes a difference in the world without quite knowing what it is doing, *there are more agents in the world than human beings alone.* Many forces, including lava flows, viruses, germs, animals, and thoughts charging through electrochemical currents across the human body-brain network, possess some characteristic of agency to some degree. And human beings possess these characteristics to a lesser extent than the most consummate ideals of autonomy, freedom, and sovereignty suggest. The creative element in agency is enabled by "litter" in the world; but litter also restricts and confines the scope of agency.[3]

Experience and Litter

James complains that "philosophers have always aimed at cleaning up the litter with which the world apparently is filled."[4] Litter is perhaps the most revealing word in this philosophy. According to *Webster's Ninth Collegiate Dictionary* litter is "decaying matter on the forest floor"; "trash, wastepaper or garbage lying scattered about"; "an untidy accumulation of objects"; or "a shabby writing desk covered with scattered articles." James may pick this word in part to note how anthropocentric the vocabulary of every philosophy is and must be. For the term is defined by contrast to human neatness and orderliness in the first instance and to human projections of order in the universe in the second. If litter is an anthropocentric projection, so are the words law, order, and neatness when applied to the world. He also picks the term to suggest that it tells us something essential about our relation to both our desks and the larger world. Our experience of the world is more comparable to the relation we have to our desks in the middle of a project than to the desk after the project has been completed. There are always subterranean energies, volatilities, and flows that exceed our formal characterizations of being. These elements either exceed the whole, if you treat the whole as the gathering of everything that exists, or they show the whole to be more than rational, smooth, or intelligible in the last instance, if you define the whole as everything that exists and subsists. Some dimensions of a pluralistic universe can be figured through terms such as litter, incompleteness, looseness, volatility, and the like. These words, again, make implicit reference to contrasting terms such as neatness, wholeness, completeness, tightness, and regularity. But while these comparisons are indeed invoked, philosophers who rely on them to prove that you must presuppose the unity of the whole even in speaking of litter in it overplay their hands. For they too have to concede that the order terms are both anthropocentric and function as vague limit terms that have not been fully fleshed out by their purveyors. The wager of those who invoke the idea of litter and the family of terms with which it is associated is that our deepest comprehension of the universe will turn out to include terms such as these as part of it. No one, to my knowledge, has so far disproven that faith or projection.

It is not that for James the whole world consists of "chance." It is rather that there is a place for something like an element of chanciness or volatility within its loose regularities and historical flows. It is not that the world is "chaotic" either, but rather that "something always escapes."[5] As far as James can see, no theology, philosophy, or science to date has marshaled sufficient resources to demonstrate that litter is removable from the whole. James makes this point when he writes that "for monism the world is . . . one great all-inclusive fact outside of which is nothing—nothing is its only alternative."[6] But he has a hard time understanding what *that* contrast term—"nothing"—means. Whatever it means, it seems to him possible to suggest that the all-inclusive fact (outside of which is nothing) includes litter. So he projects a universe in which human beings, animals, other natural forces, and a limited God are all traversed by litter, in which multiple actants make a difference as to what persists in being and what becomes.

As you probe this philosophy of pluralism it turns out to resist the conceptions of sensation, perception, and time that rationalists, conventional empiricists, and monists of other sorts often invoke. The Jamesian idea is that sensations, set in the protracted pulse of time in which they occur, *arrive already equipped with a set of preliminary connections.* There is no such thing as sense data or pure sensation. So devotees of "radical empiricism"—another phrase for a pluralistic universe in the lexicon of James—resist the assumption in which "logical empiricism" is set. They resist the abstract idea that sensations are simple, detached impressions that are nothing in particular until organized by reason. Indeed, logical empiricism presupposes an expansive idea of reason in part because it starts with an idea of pure sensations equipped with no preliminary connections from which more complex thinking and judgment proceed. With the idea of pure sensation *empiricists and rationalists themselves would have to treat the world as pure chaos unless they projected necessary categories of reason through which to organize experience.* That's why they tend to reduce the Jamesian idea of a pluralistic universe to the reductio ad absurdum of pure chaos or pure chance. That is how the philosophy of pluralism appears to them when they project the notion of pure sensation into it. That misrepresentation, in turn, is grounded in their desire to project pure sensation so that they can have simple blocks from which the unity of the whole is built.

James thus opts for a limited connectedness of being that is there from the start. This theme pulls him away from what might be called the chronological idea of time, the idea that time consists of one punctual moment after another. Of course, time can be measured that way on a clock. But *experienced time* is different from *chrono-time.* In lived experience time comes in "pulses," short bursts or flows in which a variety of elements melt into one another. The human experience of time also provides clues to how it is organized in other domains. "Time itself comes in drops," James writes.[7] In fact our experience is composed by the complex interpenetration of past, present, and future. "Past and present," James writes, drawing upon Henri Bergson, "are to some extent co-present with each other throughout experience." The only " 'present' of experience is the 'passing moment' in which the dying rearward of time and its dawning future forever mix their lights."[8]

In presenting a pluralistic universe, James folds the idea of *becoming* into it. "What really exists is not things made, but things in the making."⁹ New things come into being through time, so that the flow of time does not have either a purposive structure (the traditional philosophy of finalism) or a linear trajectory (the efficient cause of logical empiricism). Our experience is marked by feedbacks and alterations that deform continuity without eliminating it, that twist an established trajectory in new, unforeseen directions. "In the very midst of the continuity our experience comes as an alteration."¹⁰ So experience is connected, but the connections shift through alteration. Alteration and becoming enter into the very texture of time.

Of course, the preliminary experience of litter and time as alteration can be overridden by this or that faith or philosophy. But James tries to render the experiences more vivid before they are so colonized. We will soon consider the *comparative status* of the philosophy he embraces, when he takes into account contending ways of interpreting and explaining such experiences.

James is frustrated by the difficulties that he faces in describing the world he experiences. He fears that if he describes it too closely his philosophy will be captured once again by the categorical mode of presentation that marks intellectualism. And he will be pushed back toward one of the intellectualist philosophies. But it may now be possible to say, after the work of Wittgenstein, Merleau-Ponty, and Heidegger, that while James is insightful in pointing to the abundance of the world over the language through which we describe it, there is nothing in the pluralistic philosophy he advances that prevents it from finding a reasonable degree of expression *in* language. Language has rich resources. He can use it, for instance, to point to differences that exceed our capacities of description; he can identify signs indicating that which exceeds our capacities of representation; he can articulate emergent processes that exceed our capacity to predict them before they have emerged; he can creatively work upon terms in the established lexicon such as litter, pulse, pluralism, and incompleteness, stretching their traditional meanings a bit; and he can draw upon dissonant conjunctions in language such as but, moreover, however, although, nonetheless, and with, which in their cumulative effect may themselves express the philosophy of pluralism that he supports. His conception of language itself is too much under the control of the logical empiricists, formalists, and rationalists he criticizes.

The philosophy of pluralism does encounter paradox; it has not been demonstrated to be true; and it does feel implausible to many. But it is not unique in these respects. Therefore, it can be advanced as a possibility to consider; it can be articulated in ways that tap into currents of experience heretofore ignored or discredited; and its presentation can profit from creative stretching and amendments in the established terms of discourse.

James is well aware that many philosophers will resist his image of the universe, in part because it does not speak to the enterprise of philosophy as they conceive it. The task of philosophy, to them, is to articulate the most fundamental order of being in the most rigorous language available. The problem with the philosophy or faith of James, they will say, is that he makes a fetish of everyday experience, when it is precisely everyday experience that needs to be surmounted. "Philosophy, you will say, does not lie flat on its belly in the middle of experience, in the very thick of its sand and gravel . . . never getting a peep of anything from above."[11]

But maybe it should. James thinks that every philosophy does in fact start in the middle of things; it takes the cultural bearings already available to it as a point of departure. It reaches out from there; the further it reaches the more speculative and contestable it becomes. He thinks it is indeed wise to pay close attention to things *in the middle*, since you never in any event start at the very beginning or end or top or bottom. The philosophy of pluralism is presented by him as one that makes sense of fugitive dimensions of human experience left in the shadows by rationalist, monist, and dualistic philosophies. But since he also agrees—indeed insists—that his is a contestable philosophy from which others can reasonably dissent, it seems reasonable to ask: What motivates James to adopt this philosophy over other possibilities that make a claim upon his attention?

James, as we have seen, himself thinks that there is an affinity between the sensibility of a philosopher and the shape of the philosophy he or she adopts. What things in the character of James are most relevant to his philosophy of pluralism? One thing, perhaps, is how this conception of the world leaves open the possibility of new things coming into being. That makes the adventure of being intriguing to James, even as it might make it feel distressing or frightening to others. Another is the loose, though real, connection between adopting the philosophy of a pluralistic universe and actively affirming pluralism in moral and political life. It is not that you must affirm an ideal of cultural pluralism if you adopt this philosophy of the universe. You could adopt it and then conclude that in such a protean, dangerous world it is wise to keep a tight wrap on cultural life. But if you adopt the philosophy *and* also cultivate a sensibility drawn to the adventures it enables, it now becomes plausible to embrace political and ethical pluralism. You may even tap reserves of energy in you to do so over and above what it takes to maintain your identity as, say, male, Christian, heterosexual, and scientist. And you are now more apt to draw upon that energy to seek lines of connection with others who diverge from you in one way or another. So the philosophy of a pluralistic universe makes a difference to your political identity without determining it.

On James's view, an ethic is not derived in the way a conclusion is drawn from a set of premises, nor is it systematic in the way that, say, the Kantian philosophy of morality is said to be. An ethical sensibility becomes *infused* into the interests, identities, and connections that help to constitute you, stretching them in this way and limiting them in that. It is easy to see this if you consider a hypothetical person who would love to support a politics of pluralism but has been convinced by some philosophy that it is destructive of democratic unity and personal morality to do so. Such a person may encounter the philosophy of James with a sense of relief. For to *embrace* that philosophy, to love the world as you take note of the litter in it, is both to see how suffering could be reduced if you allowed a large variety of faiths to flourish in the same territorial regime and to feel the significance of acting upon that possibility. To open yourself to this philosophy and the spirituality it expresses is to take a step toward political pluralism. "Compromise and mediation," James writes in an overstatement that is insightful, "are inseparable from the pluralistic philosophy."[12]

The last motive for embracing philosophical pluralism is probably the most important to James. A philosophy of mechanical materialism forecloses space for a God to be, while traditional dualistic theologies engender a God too far removed from humanity to enable us to commune with it. James, indeed, is severe on the strictures of the latter. "The theological machinery that spoke so lovingly to our ancestors, with its finite age of the world, its creation out of nothing, its juridical morality and eschatology, its relish for rewards and punishments, its treatment of God as an external contriver, and 'intelligent and moral governer,' sounds as odd to most of us as if it were some outlandish savage religion."[13]

James suspects that the problem of evil engendered by such a faith is insurmountable. It has a hell of a time either explaining why evil exists or disconnecting its omnipotent God from responsibility for it. He also thinks it has seen its day. It is easy to see today that James overstated the second point. The "ancestral" faith has returned with a vengeance. But its very return may indicate that James was onto something in refusing to jump on the scientific-secular bandwagon and dispense with faith altogether. He thought that most human beings could not thrive unless their daily lives were infused with some sense of religious feeling. The most pressing motive working upon James to advance a pluralistic philosophy is the quest to make room for an experience of divinity that both gives faith a role in life and engages thoughtfully the most compelling historical and scientific claims of the day. He both believes that the findings of science are relevant to philosophy and doubts that those findings by themselves rule out the possibility of divinity. James, I think, would endorse Strauss's reading of Spinoza as a philosopher who failed to transcend the element of faith. But James would not approach the question of a diversity of faiths with the same unifying fervor that marks Strauss's critique of pluralism. The sensibilities of the two thinkers diverge significantly.

A pluralistic philosophy leaves the door open to a finite, loving God who participates in the world without governing it entirely. A God, perhaps, like Jesus before he was elevated to Christ by Paul and Augustine. Or like Yahweh as he appears in *The Book of J*, the oldest version of the Jewish Bible.[14] James, at any rate, embraces the conviction "that there is a God, but that he is finite, either in power or in knowledge or in both at once."[15] In doing so, he may disturb both some imperious Christians

and some overweening atheists. The interesting thing is that this pluralist poses a third option to the binary debate between them.

The Jamesian idea of a pluralistic universe speaks above all to the
highest hope that James invests in the world. The hope takes the form of
a fugitive experience of divinity that makes a powerful claim upon him:
the experience or hope that a limited God participates as one agent in a
larger world of imperfect, plural agents of different types. This is not a
God known through proof or revelation, or one clarified first and foremost through theological speculation. It is God with a small "g." It is a
god whose murmur can be heard only by those who make themselves
receptive as they listen, a god capable of inspiring and moving those who
listen to it, a god whose subsistence is consistent with bits of litter in the
universe: that is, with noise, static, zones of indiscernibility, and pools of
uncertainty out of which new and surprising entities may evolve. Not
everyone can hear this god, and many do not seek to do so. But some can,
when they let down the guardrails of everyday life and listen to the
whisper of being. Now "the threshold lowers or the valve opens, infor-
mation ordinarily shut out leaks into the mind of exceptional individuals."[16] It is a god who emerges first through the gateway of mystical
experience and is then given more specific definition through philosophical work.

The William James of A Pluralistic Universe is thus consonant with
the James of the Varieties of Religious Experience. His philosophy of a
pluralistic universe is inspired above all by his quest for a god who is
continuous with humanity. He thinks a philosophy that rules such a
possibility out altogether has one mark against it. For it rules out a
subliminal experience that many have had in numerous cultures at different moments in history when there is no absolute necessity to do so.
This philosophy makes room for a limited, loving god, even as philosophies of monism and dualism create room for different gods, and as the
mechanical materialism that James resists dismisses God as a possibility.

One attraction of James is the way he fesses up to the motives that
underlie his philosophical reflection. He does not pretend that he first
makes an airtight argument and then discovers, after the fact as it were,
that this God, that god, or no God falls into his lap.

The Status of Pluralism

James gathers various elements of lived experience—the experience of litter, the connections of sensory life, pulses of time, continuity through alteration, a mood of presumptive tolerance, and the idea of a limited god continuous with humanity without being reducible to it—into a philosophy of a pluralistic universe. But what is the status of this philosophy? If the arguments on its behalf are less than definitive, and if commitment to it is bound to the hopes you bring to its assessment, what claim can it make on those who find these arguments less than compelling or do not invest the hopes into it that James does? We have reached a critical point in the philosophy of James. It is the point at which many philosophers make claims that exceed the power of the arguments they advance. But James does not do so. He joins his philosophy of a pluralistic universe to the judgment that a variety of philosophies can and should persist in the same culture, including monist and dualist philosophies. He joins a vigorous *defense* of his philosophy to *modesty* about its status. He is a rare philosopher, breaking with the quest for certainty that haunts the tradition while refusing to relinquish the pursuit of metaphysics. This combination is apparent throughout the book, but is given its sharpest expression in the following formulation: "The only thing I emphatically insist upon is that [pluralism] is a fully coordinate hypothesis with monism. This world *may* in the last resort be a block-universe; but on the other hand it *may* be a universe only strung along, not rounded in or closed. Reality may exist distributively, just as it sensibly seems to, after all. On that possibility I do insist."[17]

James thinks he has made a strong enough case to include this philosophy in the list of viable options. He also contends that there is never a vacuum in the domain of philosophy or fundamental faith. "A conception of the world arises in you somehow, no matter how."[18] After it does, you have to decide whether to adopt it by comparison to other credible alternatives. Indeed, "deciding" is too confident and evasive a word here. You struggle with this conception in relation to others, to see where you come out. If you emerge from the struggle by embracing this view on several intercoded registers of being, you can now act in ways that help to render its plausibility more visible to others. In this way you may contribute to the shaping of the cultural life in which you participate. James himself writes that "acting thus may in certain special cases be a means of making it securely true in the end."[19] Depending on how one interprets "securely true," James may overplay his hand here. If that phrase is interpreted to mean that willing the pluralistic universe true makes it true, then it exaggerates. For if the world is a block-universe, no amount of action on other premises will change its fundamental character. But if James can be taken to mean that concerted and long-term action based upon the assumption of a pluralistic universe can help to bring into the open features of the world that would otherwise remain in the shadows, then the formulation works. Here the logic of philosophy and the character of faith move closer together, as James thinks they do in any event. You make the experience of pluralism more "securely true" by acting experimentally in several domains as if it were true. You draw what was obscure more fully into the layering of experience. "Thus do philosophy and reality, theory and action, work in the same circle indefinitely."[20]

As James's position also implies, the will to believe that helps to compose the philosophy or faith you embrace carries with it a responsibility to show respect for credible options you do not embrace. You have not, after all, proven your view beyond doubt. Neither have they. Each philosophy is confronted with loose ends, paradoxes, and uncertainties. Each has at best been shown to be one possible problematic among others.

The responsibility to show respect for credible alternatives while pushing the strengths of your own is not something simply read off from the contestable status of your commitment or faith. For you could, again, secretly acknowledge that your faith or philosophy is contestable and then use every resource at your disposal to stifle other views in your neighborhood, church, university, state, or federated union of states. One motive to do so would be to bolster self-confidence in your own faith by suppressing the expression of alternatives. So yet another augmentation in the dictum of James is needed. It consists in a call to *courage*, the courage to bear the agony of diversity in the interests of promoting the freedom of expression and curtailing the call to violence. It consists in a call to become more bicameral in your citizenship and to inspire others to do so as well.

This is where James, the soft theist, and Nietzsche, the agonistic nontheist, draw close together. The key difference between them at this point—besides the substantive difference in their conceptions of transcendence and immanence—is that Nietzsche thinks only a few will cultivate sufficient courage to "spiritualize" enmity between their faith and that of others, while James thinks that a rather large number of human beings possess such a capacity. At any rate, to embrace the persistent plurality of philosophies and creeds in life is to take a step toward translating the philosophy of a pluralistic universe into support of political pluralism. And the relation goes the other way too. To embrace the politics of pluralism can open the door to sympathetic engagement with the philosophy of a pluralistic universe promulgated by James in one way and Nietzsche in another.

These connections must not be overstated. You can be a political pluralist without endorsing the philosophical position of James. Even if you adopt a version of monism, dualism, or (non-immanent) materialism you can embrace political pluralism, *if* you admit that the philosophy you adopt, like his, is profoundly and legitimately contestable to others, and if you work upon yourself to overcome resentment of this very condition. When you acknowledge that your philosophical stance is grounded in a complex mixture of contestable faith and porous argument you take a step toward affirmation of political pluralism, even if the philosophy you embrace is block monism, strong dualism, or mechanistic materialism.

James and Contemporary Cosmology

The philosophy of a pluralistic universe has affinities with several cosmologies in the history of western philosophy. Epicurus, Lucretius, Thoreau, Nietzsche, Bergson, Whitehead, Deleuze, and Foucault are several thinkers with whom the perspective of James could be usefully compared. But let's limit ourselves for the moment to a couple of contemporary perspectives in the natural sciences. Newton and Einstein, in different ways, would dissent from the Jamesian view. Their universes are governed by general laws. But recent conceptions of science developed by Ilya Prigogine and Stephen Wolfram move closer to the position that James advanced in the early part of the twentieth century.

Prigogine, who won the Nobel Prize for inventing chaos theory, explores complex natural systems in disequilibrium. These systems grow out of the volatility in the initial conditions from which they started. And this volatility is often amplified as the system develops capacities of "self-organization" and evolves into new states of partial equilibrium. The result is an uneven trajectory of development that can be rendered intelligible retrospectively, though not predicted. Prigogine thus inserts an irreversible historical trajectory into several (though not all) systems in nature, challenging the assumption of reversibility that defined classical physics. If the system in disequilibrium is sensitive to small variations in initial conditions and contains a protean capacity for self-organization when perturbed by new forces from the outside, it contains the potential for creative evolution. The evolution of the universe, genetic mutation, biological evolution, geological patterning, climatic development, hurricanes, and human brain development all correspond to these two dictates. Moreover, the new effects generated by each system help to shape the changing environment in which other open systems develop. These changes in turn may trigger novel capacities of self-organization in them.[21] So Prigogine and his collaborator, Isabelle Stengers, challenge the regulative ideal of a closed system of explanation that traditionally informed the natural sciences, at least outside of biology. "The deterministic and reversible trajectory that we can calculate for *simple* systems . . . would require, for unstable systems, a mode of knowledge that would only make sense for [a God] . . . who knew the positions and speeds of the entities in interaction with an infinite precision (an infinite number of decimals). That being the case, is it relevant to extend to unstable dynamic systems the ideal of knowledge represented by a deterministic and reversible trajectory? Should we judge as a simple approximation the probability treatment that we *have to* apply to unstable dynamic systems, that is, judge it in the name of a knowledge that for intrinsic and noncontingent reasons we will never have?"[22]

Prigogine's perspective is remarkably close to that of James. Both postulate a degree of "litter" or "volatility of initial conditions" from which the historical trajectory of a partially open system unfolds; both play up how periodic conjunctions between two or more open systems are marked by a certain dissonance; and both emphasize how contact with new developments on the outside can spur novel capacities for self-organization on the inside.

Another, more distantly comparable perspective has recently been developed by Stephen Wolfram. Like Prigogine, Wolfram thinks that experimental science, which seeks to control the variables in experiments to test the power of possible laws of nature, is incapable of coming to terms with the *emergent character* of the most important systems in nature. They cannot be explained through simple models of linear causality. A more promising approach is to compare their development to simple computer programs that eventually, through millions of iterations, issue in patterns of complexity unpredictable before the course the iterations actually take. The order that Wolfram examines is thus an emergent order.

There are, he says, three possible sources of randomness in nature. First, the volatility of initial conditions, as we have already seen in the work of Prigogine. Second, unexpected changes in the environment that impinge upon the system in question. Third, the long-term upshot of a simple set of rules inside a system as it unfolds over time. He thinks the last is the most fundamental source of change and complexity in natural systems. As he says, "even though the underlying rules for the system are simple, and even though the system is started from simple initial conditions, the behavior that the system shows can be highly complex."[23] And "it is this basic phenomenon that is ultimately responsible for most of the complexity we see in nature."[24] The computer simulations he runs of systems that unfold with distinctive patterns of complexity after multiple iterations are utterly fascinating. He claims that the best approach to the study of nature is to ascertain which set of simple rules applies to each particular system in nature. And the best way to do that is to experiment with simple rules of different kinds, finding out what eventually issues from each set after millions of computer iterations.

Wolfram contends that human predictive capacity is systematically limited by the length of time it takes to run enough iterations of simple rules to see how they play out. He calls this "computational irreducibility." "For if meaningful general predictions are to be possible, it must at some level be the case that the system making the predictions be able to outrun the system it is trying to predict. But for this to happen the system making the predictions must be able to perform more sophisticated computations than the system it is trying to predict."[25] The most complex systems in nature are computationally irreducible because of the inordinate number of iterations that must be run to simulate them.

Wolfram also "strongly suspects," however, that it is possible to come up with a unique set of simple rules from which the universe itself has evolved. It is not clear to me how he thinks we could ever know for sure that success has been achieved, since we are stuck in the universe and it has not yet reached its end-state. He wants to see around a corner that has not yet been turned. He seems to think that if a simple set of rules could track the universe to this point we would be in an excellent position to extrapolate from them. He does acknowledge that even if you could be confident about the underlying set of rules you would not be in a position to say *why* this set stands at the base of the evolution rather than another set.

At any rate, Wolfram's entertainment of *the hope* to find simple rules governing the evolution of the universe defines both the similarity and the difference between his perspective and that of James. The similarity resides in the implicit connection that he acknowledges between hope and philosophy. The difference can be seen by pointing to the distance between James's conception of God and the conception that Wolfram would pursue if he chose to do so. For James, God is a limited force operating in conjunction with a plurality of other forces. For Wolfram a God, if it subsisted, would be both the originator of the first set of simple rules and the one agent who could give an authoritative answer to why that set rather than another was inaugurated. Such a God, for James, is too all-knowing and separate from us to be congruent with the subliminal communication that James experiences and prizes. It is also incongruent with the experience of litter in the world.

James's position suggests to me the possibility of forging a synthesis between Prigogine and Wolfram, rather than simply selecting one theory over the other. Such a synthesis would make it possible to identify three sources of randomness and complexity in dissonant conjunction: volatility in initial conditions; the long-term upshot of rules; and surprising changes in the external environment that trigger latent capacities of self-organization in a system. It is when you imagine these three sources periodically impinging upon each other that you move close to the Jamesian vision of a pluralistic universe. There are places in Wolfram's study where he approaches such a vision too. The recent work by the biologist of complexity Brian Goodwin seems to me to head in this direction as well, as he explores the kind of order that arises "spontaneously" in complex systems.[26]

The biggest difference between James and Wolfram, however, is in the temper that each displays when the most speculative and uncertain parts of his theory are advanced. Wolfram's text is replete with phrases such as "I strongly suspect" and "I strongly believe." These terms admit the element of speculation in his theory while simultaneously implying that it is incumbent upon reflective people visiting these programs to accept the speculation that he attaches to them. Wolfram resists pluralism in science, as when he writes, "And all of this supports my strong belief that in the end it will turn out that every detail of our universe does indeed follow rules that can be represented by a very simple program—and that everything we see will ultimately emerge just from running this program."[27]

James doubts that we will arrive there "in the end." He treats his theory as a reasonable projection that *can* be believed given the evidence but by no means *must* be believed. He articulates such a modest position partly because it reflects his considered faith in relation to available evidence and partly because he suspects that every interpretation in the natural sciences, human sciences, philosophy, and theology is invested somewhere with a speculative vision. It is best to lay as many of these cards on the table as you can, even if some of them will remain hidden until a new, unexpected theory comes along to throw them into relief. But given the problematical character of such speculations, it is also wise to do so in ways that acknowledge the credibility of other possibilities too. James cannot specify in advance the outside limit of "the other possibilities"; he knows that new evidence, new technologies of exploration, and new theoretical speculation might throw some currently credible options into disarray. For instance, the computer that Wolfram relies upon was not even on the horizon of possibility when James wrote. Who knows what effects it would have had upon the theories of Einstein, Heisenberg, Nietzsche, and James had it been? And new technologies in the future might become pertinent to the theory of Wolfram.

So James presents his faith-speculation as a reasonable possibility, one in which he is profoundly invested and one which informs his life. James expresses the temper of a deep pluralist, as he advances the defensible, contestable speculation that the universe itself is pluralistic.

Pluralism and Care for the World

James would have been taken with the discovery by Lynn Margulis of a strange operation called symbiogenesis.[28] Symbiogenesis is the process by which a bit of DNA from one bacterium escapes into the surrounding liquid. Sometimes it travels to another bacterium, creating a crisis of survival for that bacterium because of its different metabolic composition. Often the invaded bacterium perishes. But occasionally a creative process of self-organization is activated in the second bacterium in response to the intrusion, triggering the genesis of a new kind of bacterium, one with a nucleus. This emergent is the result neither of a mutation nor of the sexual exchange of genetic material. It is the chancy effect of an invasion, which occasionally triggers a creative response by the invaded cell. The first nucleated bacterium that emerged eons ago from such a chancy conjunction provided the base from which biological evolution itself proceeded. Unless symbiogenesis occurred at the inception of the evolutionary process, there would be no plants, insects, rain forests, vertebrates, cloud cover, human beings, or platypuses today.

To James and Margulis the swimming DNA is litter in motion; it is noise or static detached from any stable pattern of repetition. Out of the creative conjunction between the escaped material and the response of the host, something new emerged. Emergent causation, you might call it. Sometimes, as in this instance, the emergent sets the stage for yet later innovations. James would call this process a rich example of creative indeterminism in motion. Unlike the philosophy of determinism, which decrees that once the basic elements of the universe are laid down every new or novel process is determined in advance, "Indeterminism . . . says that the parts have a certain amount of loose play on one another, so that the laying down of one of them does not necessarily determine what the others shall be. It admits that possibilities may be in excess of actualities, and that things not yet revealed to our knowledge may really in themselves be ambiguous . . . Indeterminism thus denies the world to be one unbending unit of fact. It says there is a certain ultimate pluralism in it . . . To that view actualities seem to float in a larger sea of possibilities from out of which they are chosen."[29]

This "loose play" between elements is the medium of "indeterminism," or better, *emergent causation* in nature. In a process of emergent causation the novel concatenation of disparate elements on occasion issues in something new, which could not have been predicted before it came into being and may set the stage for other unpredictable emergents in the future. Emergent causation participates in creative evolution rather than mechanical evolution.

Note too the word "chosen" at the end of the quotation from James. The loose play referred to by James operates in nonhuman nature as well as human-centered processes. The word "chosen" seems to point to a series of affinities and resonances between human and nonhuman processes. James does not invest agency entirely in humans while divesting it altogether from nonhuman processes. Chemicals, minerals, and electrical currents enter into the composition of our being. These processes carry an energetic element of loose play in them; and our own experiences of complex decision making, choice, will, experimentation, and the like may be imbued with selective *affinities* to those primordial processes. Certainly, the loose play in the former processes preceded and conditioned it in us. It is because of the loose energy in nature that we may feel a host of affinities and connections to the larger world in which we are set. Such feelings occur at different levels of awareness and degrees of complexity, depending upon the affinities in question.

The rationalist division of the world into "subjects" and "objects" represses such affinities, insulating our consciousness from the world that courses through, over, and around us. The delicate zone "in between" subjects of action and objects acted upon must be articulated with caution. But Jamesian philosophy attends to a series of affinities and interdependencies between us and the pluralistic universe. Some of these connections are immediately felt, at different levels of awareness. Others must be theorized before they are appreciated, as James has done; then they too can enter into our feeling for the world. The lines of difference between human beings and the rest of nature now become multiple rather than singular, and distributive rather than categorical. Each difference now comes equipped with a corollary connection. Our capacities to think, feel, see, smell, choose, deliberate, speak, and innovate are prefigured in other sectors of the world; and some of these capacities in us are exceeded elsewhere. Since ethical life, for James, is more a matter of inspiration and attraction than command and obedience, the point is to encourage this feeling of interspecies connection across a broad array of differences.

Molten lava flowing from a volcano eventuates in complex granite formations because of the different rates of cooling of the diverse elements. "Granite forms out of cooling magma, a viscous fluid composed of a diversity of molten materials. Each has a different threshold of crystallization. And those that solidify earlier serve as containers for those that acquire a crystal form later. The result is a complex set of heterogeneous crystals that interlock with one another, and that is what gives granite its superior strength."[30]

Each granite formation acquires its distinctive strength from this process of differential cooling and containing; and each crystallization of lava into granite exhibits a unique pattern that is neither predictable in advance nor replicable. The result may suggest an analogy to the evolution of a small town into the topsy-turvy shape of a large city. Some people who love granite may thus find themselves doubly attracted to cities. This attraction grows as they study the complexities and indeterminacies of granite crystallization, comparing it to the checkered history by which the byways of a city were formed. Attention to such affinities may bind you to both cities and granite more deeply than you otherwise would be to either. Better, the color of your perception of each becomes inhabited by your attraction to the other. If lava flows and granite were to disappear from the face of the earth, our appreciation of the complexity of cities might diminish. And vice versa. And if similar disappearances were repeated in other such circuits of connection, our sensibilities themselves would become impoverished. Our very capacity for analogy would be depleted. It might feel like living in Texas.

In a pluralistic universe, care for the world emerges from the multiplication of such circuits. Granite-city circuits, circuits between human innovation and apes who invent new cultural activities, circuits between the volatility of a tornado and that of a God who speaks out of a whirlwind, circuits between the rail map of England and the body-brain circuits of human beings, circuits between parrots who change the subject while speaking and the creative element in human language.[31]

Or take the huge cockroach I found stalking my kitchen one day when I was a visitor at the Australian National University. It felt imperative to eliminate this surprisingly large creature from my living space. When it smelled or saw that I was trying to kill it, it anticipated every move I was about to make in an uncanny way, leaping around in erratic, purposive ways. After what felt like a half-hour of mortal combat, it seemed to be crushed under the magazine I had pounded down on it (in one of my "creative" maneuvers). I lifted up the magazine in anticipatory disgust, expecting to observe a mashed cockroach. But it was not there. Stunned, I looked every which way, sensing at some level that I had now become the hunted one. Just as I was about to give up the search my eye caught a glimmer of brown squeezed into a tiny crevice between the cupboard counter and the wall. It was barely visible to my crude eye. As soon as my eye touched it, it reinitiated our hand-to-tentacle combat. An instinct of intelligent survival, activated in numerous ways. One I have recognized in myself from time to time in emergency situations—one, indeed, I even felt a trace of during minor combat with that intense, creative bug. An affinity of affect between two diverse beings in a world populated by innumerable such affinities across multiple lines of difference.

Henri Bergson, who formed a mutual admiration society with James, suggests, "There is no manifestation of life which does not contain, in a rudimentary state—latent or potential—the essential characters of most other manifestations. The difference is in the proportions." He even says that "there is not a single property of vegetable life that is not found, in some degree, in certain animals; not a single characteristic feature of the animal that has not been seen in certain species at certain moments in the vegetable world."[32] A world marked by multiple, uncanny affinities across large differences. You might kill an oversized cockroach that disturbed your sense of apartment propriety while later evincing new respect for the creative intensity of the species.

According to the feeling-imbued philosophy of a pluralistic universe, to care about the diversity of humanity writ large is to take a step toward caring about the larger world that courses through and around us. It is to care about litter in motion in the creativity of a cockroach, the fecundity of rainforests, lava flows, swimming DNA, the sonority of the human voice, turbulent water flows, and the human body-brain-culture network. Above all, it is to care about that delicate balance between creativity and stability that enables nature and civilizations to change while maintaining themselves. To appreciate the element of energetic uncertainty circulating through the world is to cultivate cautious solicitude for the world.

Neither James nor I support that strange variant of academicism he calls "intellectualism." We neither intend to construct and defend an entire system of ethics through argument alone nor seek to separate ethical principles from sensuous feeling. Nor do we buy those closed schemes of explanation advanced by many in the social sciences. To us, care for the world follows neither from a set of sufficient moral principles you are obligated to obey nor from a mode of knowledge that enables us in principle to explain the world completely. James writes in an inspirational and attractional mode rather than an imperative style. Better, he mixes a large dose of the former element into the light texture of the second. He seeks to enliven our feelings of connection with the world, partly by endowing it with more capacities than his recent predecessors tended to do. He has outgrown the philosopher's illusion that argument alone is sufficient to thinking, ethical life, and politics. The Jamesian feeling for the world, if it is communicated to us, becomes sedimented into our interests, identities, responsibilities, and principles, deepening them in one way and stretching them in another. To cultivate an ethical disposition of connectedness across difference is to refine our capacities of feeling.

Philosophers in the Kantian tradition, who separate sensuality from ethical life and demand a systematic moral theory, find the Jamesian orientation perplexing. To them it is unacceptable to fold "heteronomous" elements such as affect, feeling, desire, and passion into morality. But from the Jamesian viewpoint, as you come to appreciate the interconnectedness of things and the obdurate element of uncertainty and creativity in their trajectories, multiple lines of affinity between them and us begin to find expression inside your ideas of self-interest, explanation, identity, identification, obligation, and responsibility. It is possible to give arguments of self-interest in favor of protecting biological diversity, closing holes in the ozone layer, curtailing nuclear power, reducing water and soil pollution, and purifying the air. But unless a protean care for the world is mixed into the conception of self-interest, more insulated definitions of human need are apt to win the day. As you come to feel this larger web of loose affinities and uncertain connections, you outgrow the implicit idea that the world was designed for us alone, or that human beings can master it entirely, or that we can in principle know it completely, or that morality is reducible to the deduction of pure obligations from abstract principles, or that we can insulate ourselves from the rest of the world. At any rate, the philosophy of a pluralistic universe calls each of these assumptions into question. It suggests that human civilization is an event that might not have happened, and that it is most apt to survive if we attend to the fecundity, volatility, and complexity of interconnections in which it is set.

Interlude

—Sometimes you hear that the bicameral orientation to citizenship appropriate to pluralism really means relativism. It would be difficult to convince innumerable pluralists of that who have put themselves on the line to fight against aggressive, unitarian movements.

—A conception of the world arises in you somehow, no matter how.[1]

—When your faith is disturbed your being is rattled. You react bodily through the roiling of your gut, the hunching of your shoulders, the pursing of your lips, and the tightening of your skin.

—The problem of evil *within* faith flows from the dissonant conjunction between the *layering of faith* into the body-brain circuits of the faithful and the *relational character of faith* in a world marked by numerous faiths.

—The orthodox premise cannot be refuted by experience nor by recourse to the principle of contradiction. An indirect proof of this is that Spinoza and his like owed such success as they had . . . against orthodoxy to laughter and mockery . . .[2]

—The genuine refutation of orthodoxy would require the proof that the world and human life are perfectly intelligible without the assumption of a mysterious God . . . But to grant that revelation is possible means to grant that the philosophic account and the philosophic way of life are not necessarily, not evidently, the true account and the right way of life; philosophy, the quest for evident and necessary knowledge, rests itself on an unevident decision . . . , just as faith. Hence the antagonism between Spinoza and Judaism, between belief and unbelief, is ultimately not theoretical, but moral.[3]

—This light recoil upon the relational dimension of your own faith is embraced in order to become more ethical in a fast-paced world. It is part of the process by which the ritual dimension of faith is honored even as the civic virtues of deep pluralism are folded into relational practice.

—Philosophers have always aimed at cleaning up the litter with which the world apparently is filled.[4]

—The pluralistic view which I prefer to adopt is willing to believe that there may ultimately never be an all-form at all, that the substance of reality may never get totally connected, that some of it may remain outside the largest combination of it ever made, and that a distributive form of reality, the each-form, is logically as acceptable, and empirically as probable, as the all-form commonly acquiesced in as so obviously the self-evident thing.[5]

—The national image of a centered majority around which minorities revolve is transfigured into the image of interdependent minorities on several registers of being, each of which needs to sustain connections with numerous others to generate practices of common governance.

—Past and present are to some extent coexisting throughout experience. The only 'present' of experience is the 'passing moment' in which the dying rearward of time and its dawning future forever mix their lights.[6]

—An ethic is not derived in the way a conclusion is drawn from a set of premises, nor is it systematic in the way that, say, the Kantian philosophy of morality is said to be. An ethical sensibility becomes *infused* into the interests, identities, and connections that help to constitute you, stretching them in one way and limiting them in another.

—The deterministic and reversible trajectory that we can calculate for *simple* systems . . . would require, for unstable systems, a mode of knowledge that would only make sense for [a God] . . . who knew the

positions and speeds of the entities in interaction with an infinite precision (an infinite number of decimals). That being the case, is it relevant
to extend to unstable dynamic systems the ideal of knowledge represented by a deterministic and reversible trajectory?[7]

—This world *may* in the last resort, be a block-universe; but on the
other hand it *may* be a universe only strung-along, not rounded in or
closed. Reality may exist distributively just as it sensibly seems to, after
all. On that possibility I do insist.[8]

—There is no manifestation of life which does not contain in a
rudimentary state—latent or potential—the essential characters of most
other manifestations. The difference is in the proportions . . . [T]here is
not a single property of vegetable life that is not found, in some degree,
in certain animals; not a single characteristic feature of the animal that
has not been seen in certain species at certain moments in the vegetable
world.[9]

—In a pluralistic universe care for the world emerges from the multiplication of such circuits. Granite-city circuits, circuits between human
innovation and apes who invent new cultural activities, circuits between
the volatility of a tornado and that of a God who speaks out of a whirlwind, circuits between the rail map of England and the body-brain circuits of human beings, circuits between parrots who change the subject
while speaking and the creative element in human language.

—It is possible to give arguments of self-interest in favor of protecting biological diversity, closing holes in the ozone layer, curtailing nuclear power, reducing water and soil pollution, and purifying the air. But
unless a protean care for the world is mixed into the conception of self-
interest, more insulated definitions of human need are apt to win the
day. As you come to feel this larger web of loose affinities and uncertain
connections, you may outgrow the implicit idea that the world was designed for us alone, or that human beings can master it entirely, or that
we can in principle know it completely, or that morality is reducible to
the deduction of pure obligations from abstract principles, or that we can
insulate ourselves from the rest of the world.

—So often in the past . . . , reality had disappointed me because at the
instant my senses perceived it my imagination . . . could not apply itself
to it, in virtue of that ineluctable law which ordains that we can only

imagine what is absent. And now, suddenly, the effect of this harsh law had been neutralized, temporarily annulled, by a marvelous experience of nature which had caused a sensation . . . to be mirrored at one and the same time in the past, so that my imagination was permitted to savor it, and in the present, where the actual shock to my senses . . . had added to the dreams of the imagination the concept of "existence" which they usually lack, and through this subterfuge had made it possible for my being to secure, to isolate, to immobilize—for a moment brief as a flash of lightning—what normally it never apprehends: a fragment of time in the pure state.[10]

CHAPTER 4

PLURALISM
AND TIME

Punctuality and Memory Waves

I check my watch often. I am on time for most appointments. I start and end classes at the appointed moment, shucking off announcements not closely tied to the intellectual issue at hand. I never miss a train or plane. And when I go for a run I hit the timer button at the beginning and end of the course, checking the result as if I were still in competition. Despite what some theorists of "lived time" may suggest, clock time today forms a critical part of lived time. The "Timex Ironman," and its divisions into hours, minutes, seconds, and tenths of seconds, enters into the minutiae of experience. That experience would be different if we measured time officially with a sundial and tacitly by reference to the sun's location in the sky. Such a clock would function well in a world without closely coordinated train schedules, punch-in clocks, plane departures, class starting times, track records, prescribed lunch breaks, the twenty-four-second rule in NBA basketball, and pub hours. People like me glance at our watches when others arrive "late" for lunch, class, or a movie date. We can be a pain. But the watch, at least, is on our side.

Clock time is coordinated with a schematic experience of space. I started class at eleven o'clock in Dotson Hall; we had a noon lunch at the One World Cafe; my "record" was set as I ran around the reservoir on September 12th. In fact, we regularly use spatial metaphors to articulate temporal experience.[1] "Put that *behind* you"; "I'm looking *ahead* to the vacation"; "don't worry about the *distant* future"; "the deadline is *here*"; "the delivery date is still *far away*." Merleau-Ponty would say that the character of human embodiment suggests these articulations. We stand upright as we walk, with our eyes facing forward, stepping last on our toes as they bend upward, in a way that makes it easy to coordinate that which is "in front of us" with the future toward which we are heading. If we moved differently in bodies otherwise organized, these coordinations would not be so effortless. It would be rough to have your toes at the back of your feet, your eyes sunk into the top of your head, and your knees facing in different directions. Such a combination would also complicate the coordination between space and time now incorporated into experience.

Henri Bergson contends that the ubiquity of clock time, the particular shape of our embodied motility, and the interested character of action combine to organize perception in action-oriented ways. Everyday perception does not represent the world as it is before we encounter it. It organizes experience in the interests of potential modes of action. Perception *subtracts* and *contracts* the abundant material flooding the senses until a conduct-oriented snapshot has been set in a homogeneous image of space and time. Such a practice of perception, Bergson says over and over, is indispensable to life. But it provides an impoverished basis from which to plunge into the tacit experience of duration also available to us, or to do philosophy. Rationalism and classical empiricism, diverging from each other in notable ways, nonetheless concur in building upon the results of operational perception rather than plunging into the activity of life as perception itself crystallizes. As a result, advocates of each view come up with images of space, cause, time, morality, and politics that work reasonably well in dealing with stable relations set in persisting contexts. But each functions poorly in a setting pluralized by significant differences of collective memory or an unexpected conjunction of events that turns the flow of time in a novel direction. We caught a glimpse of a more complex image of time when we allowed James to coordinate the idea of a pluralistic universe with the idea of time as that which flows in "pulses." It is now time to allow Bergson to develop this idea more fully.

Clock time encourages you to think of past, present, and future as separate and discrete. First I heard the alarm ring, now I am shaving, then I will drive to work. Fair enough. But durational time, as I will call it, exceeds this experience, even as it enters into communication with it. Let us approach the difference by reviewing a brief, imaginary conversation. The words in quotes are those of the two parties in conversation. Those in parentheses compose an interior dialogue of one of the parties as the conversation proceeds:

> X: "I should go to Mike's funeral. He was a good friend. But Cheryl is not feeling well, and work is pressing."

> (Y: Alan's funeral . . . I had made the plane reservation to see him one more time. But then the call came . . . Why didn't I reschedule and attend the funeral? To console his family and friends, and to accept their consolations. But no, I sat around the house, pining for my friend alone.)

> Y: "How close a friend was he? Do you know his family?"

> (X commences an interior dialogue unknown to Y, drawing upon a series of memories as he does.)

> X: "Mike and I were close . . . When I was getting started I stood in awe of him. Once I taught a class with him. Better, we pretended to co-teach, but he taught and I learned . . ."

> (Y: Alan's friends were cool after that. Not that I saw them much. I don't blame them now. My mother . . .

That taught the lesson . . . The relatives and friends who consoled *us* . . . Did she *know* she was going to die when she made that last visit? It wasn't like her to travel so far. She squeezed back once when I held her hand at the hospital. But no words could cross her lips by then . . . Why are tears welling up? Don't cry! *His* friend is the one who just died, for God's sake . . .)

Y: "Are there other people you know who will attend?"

(Y: My partner, my kids. Should we discuss our impending deaths? Mom didn't say anything. It's too maudlin . . .)

X: "You know, I've got to go to this funeral. . . ."

A brief conversation. Many of the memories of Y (in parentheses) flood into attention as X speaks. Y both listens to X and relives a sheet of his own past as he does. His attention extends to past and future alike, not as the past was when experienced but as it arrives now in the interstices of this conversation. A conversation in which past and future coexist in a protracted present stretching out to both. A "crystal of time," as Deleuze might put it, in which the disjointedness of time itself, with its differentiation into presents that pass and pasts that are preserved, becomes palpable. The present could not be without protraction. It would be an empty instant, like the flick of a second on a Timex. Memories bubble up as they will, feeding into the conversation without becoming objects of it. This happens not merely to Y, but to X too. His parents and friends may enter the fray, as well as his colleagues and children.

The memories alluded to in that short conversation take the shape of unstated recollections. But for a memory to cross the point at which it is called up as recollection, it must have already arrived near the tipping point. It was not plucked immediately out of a huge storehouse covering every event in Y's life. It was crystallized from a *wave of memory* called into the vicinity by the conversation. Most of that wave subsists below the threshold of explicit recollection. A slight shift in the conversation might call up some of these. Say X brings up his father's death and the regret he has about the way he dealt with it. A new set of recollections might flood over Y, some of which had already been pressing against his small chamber of consciousness because of the preceding things said. Memories that subsist below recollection are virtual in that they might have effects on the flow of the conversation but do not themselves assume the shape of articulated thoughts. You can call these memories without recollection. Some virtual memories possess the potential to become recollections at another moment. Others might color the conversation but are not full enough to be brought into articulation at any point, even if there were ample time for them to be. They are like the infrasound we encounter everyday: its vibrations affect our moods, feelings, perceptions, and judgments while operating below the threshold of hearing.[2] Perhaps the wave of memory that the conversation calls up in Y includes an embodied trace of being coddled by his mother before he could speak, just as he feels those tears welling up. The vibrations constituting that inframemory fall below the threshold of articulateness susceptible in principle to explicit recollection. So we can now identify at least three layers of memory at work in the same conversation.

Duration is this rapid flow back and forth between several layers of past and future anticipation as a perception, conversation, action, judgment, or reminiscence crystallizes. Duration is time perdured and endured. It is a continuous pulse of time, with each element shading into the others and melting into them in turn. The conversation may take five minutes in clock time; but it could roll back and forth across thirty-five years in durational time. Bergson says that duration lurks in the shadows of punctual time. He seeks to render vivid "the self which endures" percolating within the self that perceives:

> When, with the inner regard of my consciousness, I examine my person in its passivity, like some superficial encrustment, first I perceive all the perceptions which come to it from the material world. These perceptions are clear-cut, distinct, juxtaposed or mutually juxtaposable; they seek to group themselves into objects. Next I perceive memories more or less adherent to those perceptions and which serve to interpret them;

these memories are, so to speak, as if detached from
the depths of my person and drawn to the periphery by
perceptions resembling them; they are fastened to me
without being absolutely myself. And finally, I become
aware of tendencies, motor habits, a crown of virtual
actions more or less solidly bound to those perceptions
and these memories . . . Turned outwards from within,
together they constitute the surface of a sphere which
tends to expand and lose itself in the external world.
But if I pull myself in from the periphery toward the
center, if I seek deep down within me what is the most
uniformly, the most constantly, and durably myself,
I find something altogether different.[3]

What you find beneath these encrustations "is a continuity of flow
comparable to no other flowing . . . , a succession of states each one of
which announces what follows and contains what precedes." The continuity speaks to how they "all dovetail into one another."[4] But there is
also alteration within this continuity. One memory called up during an
encounter may twist or turn the thought, conversation, or act in a new
direction. As when X says, as if from nowhere, "I need to reconsider
this . . ." Duration is the flow of time as becoming. It is waves of memory
protracted into a present unfolding toward an altered future.

"Inner duration is the continuous life of a memory which prolongs
the past into the present, whether the present distinctly contains the
every growing image of the past or whether, by its continual changing of
quality, it attests rather to the increasingly heavy burden dragged along
behind one the older one grows."[5]

We have already seen enough to appreciate how in a pluralistic
society people are both linked by fate and separated by diversities of age
and experience, sunk into divergent layers of memory, perception, judgment, and action. Perception, judgment, and action can be intense because affect clings to the memories that help to constitute them and the
anticipations that flow from them. Politics does not begin after those
issues are settled. It sinks into memory, perception, judgment, and action. It dips into the affectively imbued experience of duration.

Time as Becoming

Duration, says Bergson, is "the very mobility of being."[6] The mobility of being, moreover, exceeds our participation in it. It runs through the stretch of a thought in the midst of crystallizing, a conversation, the ebb and flow of an electoral campaign, the emergence of capitalism out of feudalism, dramatic climatic changes, the bumpy course of biological evolution, the growth of new geological formations, and the evolution of the universe. Any relatively open system with significant capacities of self-organization participates to some degree in durational time, even though human beings are the only ones we have encountered to date who can, albeit with difficulty, plunge into this experience and render it a bit more vivid to themselves. The world of things we perceive—once you place each thing on the appropriate scale of duration—is a world of multiple "becomings."

This is the juncture at which Bergson—the philosopher of a continually creating, limited God in a world marked by "creative evolution"—meets Nietzsche—the nontheistic philosopher of world as becoming.[7] Time is becoming. And becoming is time in an open cosmos. It is through becoming that the new surges into being. Separate trajectories of becoming, set on different scales of clock time, periodically collide, clash, collude, and melt into each other, issuing in unpredictable changes: a new idea, a new faith, an unexpected candidate, a new economy, an ice age, a novel species, the consolidation of a mountain range, the emergence of matter. Let us, this time around, focus on the points of *contact* between a philosophy of immanence and a philosophy with a trace of transcendence. Let us do so with respect to becoming.

Two elements are critical to time as becoming. First, duration unfolds in an entity with some capacity for self-organization or autopoeisis. Second, a change in one field of becoming can open up new exchanges with other partially open systems, set on different scales of clock time. Out of the encounter new things might flow, bubble, or burst into being, for good or ill. How could the new formations be explained or predicted in advance, if those immersed in the politics of alteration themselves do not even have a well-defined concept of them before their emergence?

Such conceptions emerge after the fact, as it were. World capitalism might be spurred to a new level or ground down to something heretofore unknown by a dramatic shift in the climate; the emergence of a new virus or bacterium might pave the way for development of a new medicine or a plague that overtakes humanity; the invention of the computer and consolidation of the internet (both tied to state military projects), in conjunction with a new intensification of religious conflicts, might issue in a cross-state network of terrorist cells capable of unsettling the system of state governance and capitalist process; a new messiah, emerging out of historic dissonances between Judaism, Christianity, and Islam, might challenge the hegemony of each. For it would be surprising if we had seen the last major religion erupt on the face of the earth.

A world of becoming is a world that exceeds human explanation or control. The possible points of fateful contact between emergent formations are too immense for either. Anxiety about that immensity, indeed, subtends several efforts in philosophy, journalism, theology, the natural sciences, and the social sciences to occlude, deny, or suppress awareness that we inhabit a world of becomings that pass by, collide, and collude. That is one reason, perhaps, why the experience of duration is often ignored.

Bergson thinks that if we focus upon fugitive experiences of becoming in human life we will be in a better position to appreciate how the world writ large also participates in becoming. When we dip into duration, we dimly feel its creativity at work: "we see that it means creation, and that if that which is being made endures, it can only be because it is inseparably bound to what is making itself."[8] This fugitive experience, so easy to forget while responding to the demands of operational perception, tenure clocks, and the shortness of life, sets a base point from which to connect with several nonhuman processes. If numerous processes and beings in the world, including turbulent water flows, cells, bacteria, lava flows, tornadoes, human beings, biological evolution, and the evolution of the universe contain differential capacities for self-"making"—that is, modes of self-organization not entirely reducible to efficient causation—and if these open systems periodically encounter changes in other modes of becoming to which they are linked, then we inhabit a world in which "the future is not altogether determined at the present moment."[9] We inhabit a world of becoming in which each mode of becoming is connected to others on different scales of chrono-time.

Of course, no one has proven that Bergson is right on this score. Perhaps someday every complex process will be covered by cleanly delineated modes of efficient causation between distinct "factors" incongruent with Bergsonian themes of duration, creation, and the new. On the other hand, we may increasingly find ourselves revising classical conceptions of causality until they incorporate room for real novelty and creation.[10] The latter is the direction that Bergson, Nietzsche, William James, Ilya Prigogine, and Gilles Deleuze pursue in their different ways.[11] I cannot hope to resolve this debate definitively. I will merely strive to render the Bergsonian image of time palpable by reconfiguring the analogies implicitly invoked when people think about the flow of time. While many extrapolate from the observation of simple processes to complex formations, promising that the latter will *eventually* be explicable in the same way as the former, Bergson inverts that extrapolation. He seeks to move from the fugitive human experience of duration to the other processes. I join him in this endeavor, treating activities such as thinking, following a movie plot with strange twists, and listening to a melody to provide hints applicable to several domains. Thinking, remember, is part of this world. If it is irreducible to a pattern of linear causality, and if it helps to usher new things and possibilities into the world, then is it not reasonable to treat *this worldly activity* as a sign that other processes, in their specific ways, do so too? It would seem so, unless you seek either to reduce thinking to efficient causality or to place it above the world. The latter strategy is the one followed by many post-Kantians, as they first accept uncritically much of the classical image of science and then transcendentalize thinking to protect it from succumbing to that reduction.

Neither Nietzsche nor Bergson does that. Nietzsche binds the idea that the flow of worldly time is creative to a faith that the universe has evolved without either guidance by a god or obedience to a set of closed laws of determination. Indeed, he thinks that the latter faith is another version of the former. He admits no trace of transcendence, hence no divine guarantor, either of a world governed by laws in the last instance or of a close fit between human capacities of discernment and the structure of the world. He does not object to the idea of laws as loose approximations of a more protean world. Such summaries can be most useful. But the very idea of tight "laws" of nature reflects to him the remains of an old theology that most scientists purport to dismiss. It seems likely that a godless world would be organized with, as James puts it, a lot of litter in it that exceeds the lawlike approximations we discern. Bergson bolsters his preliminary image of creative time with faith in a continually creative God who energizes numerous media in the world while depending upon them to continue the process of creation in an open universe. He admits that his faith is contestable. As he writes, "Here we are in the field of probabilities alone. But we cannot reiterate too often that philosophic certainty admits of degrees, that it calls for intuition as well as for reason."[12] Nietzsche speaks of the immanence of becoming, in "a Dionysian world of the eternally self-creating, the eternally self-destroying"; that which becomes is never entirely reducible to the nondivine sources from which it springs, partly because of how it is deflected, absorbed, and otherwise modified by other entities and processes.[13] He also acknowledges this image to be a "conjecture" rather than a certainty. The fugitive inspiration of transcendence to which Bergson refers and the energy of immanence to which Nietzsche refers operate in uncannily similar ways. Both thinkers could accede to this general statement by Bergson, who points to "an energy to which no limit can be assigned." Bergson's transcendence is not "a closed concept, still less a definition of God such as might enable us to conclude what the world is like or what it should be like."[14]

One difference between the two concerns is whether a vague purpose may operate within time as becoming. This difference, between attention to the fugitive pressures of immanence and attention to the fugitive whisper of transcendence, may never be resolved definitively, even if it makes a difference to life which way we opt on the issue. But it is perhaps more important today to dwell for a time, as we have been doing, inside the subtle points of convergence between one image of becoming bound to the fugitive forces of immanence and another attuned to the mystical whisper of transcendence. Both contest the sufficiency of chrono-time and strong finalism.

The Dissonance of Time

How might one become more attuned to a world of interdependent, dissonant becomings, periodically meshing to consolidate new states of equilibrium? One way that Bergson himself discounted is through engagement with film. He thought the new medium too "mechanical" to do the job. Film, however, has now become a promising candidate for that very task, partly because it draws noise, music, rhythm, words, and image into creative conjunctions, and partly because it assumes the flow of a "motion picture." *Time Code* may provide a timely case in point. This film, directed in 2000 by Mike Figgis, was shot with four hand-held cameras, each rolling in real clock time without breaks or cuts. It is marked by none of the flashbacks, depth-of-field shots, wide-angle shots, irrational cuts, or lingering close-ups through which other films intensify the experience of becoming already simmering in experience. Still, it does a lot of work.

The screen is divided into four frames. The two-eyed, two-eared viewer with one stomach is given the impossible task of negotiating sound and movement in all four frames simultaneously, as each frame rolls along in real clock time. At first you feel overwhelmed and confused, as if you had entered an unfamiliar country. How could you track everything in each frame? Then you focus first on this frame, then on that one. The film helps by increasing the decibel level in one frame that had been relatively quiet for a while, and by periodically heightening the volatility of movement in another in which there had been relative quiescence. But its help is a liability in another way, for it draws you away from quiet and slow things elsewhere that might later prove pertinent. Just as you are settling into this new viewing experience the action begins to circulate across two or more frames, carried by vehicles such as walking, a car, cell phone calls, a wiretap, resounding noises, earthquake tremors, and a gunshot. After a time, you may experience the illusion that you are watching, listening, and responding to the action in all four frames at once, observing an open whole that is becoming.

The intersecting stories that compose the film are linked first and foremost by harsh tremors that shake the ground beneath the feet of the participants on several occasions, unnerving them in different ways at the same times. Each time a tremor interrupts something important going on in two or three frames, drawing some figures closer together and intensifying the uncertainties and anxieties that had already begun to divide others. Who knows what virtual memories are pulled to the tipping point by the conjunction between a tremor and some conversation? But if you attend to the altered set of Emma's face as she strolls slowly down the street in the upper right frame, it is clear that something new has been called into being by the conjunction of a tremor, the difficulties with her unreliable husband Alex, and the half-audible session she has just finished with her therapist.

As the participants endure these moments, new connections are made with strangers, and old uncertainties become translated into new disconnections that could not have been predicted. Each small and large shift is then carried into the next set of engagements. As happens with Lauren, the suspicious, rich lover who has dropped her partner Rose off to audition for a part in a film. She has to endure one of the worst tremors alone, as she also addresses her suspicions about Rose.

At one point Lauren is listening attentively in the top left frame to the wire she has planted on Rose. Rose is having sex with Alex—the man Rose hopes will get her the audition she told Lauren was now to be taking place—in the bottom right frame. But Lauren can't make out what is happening because the sounds of lovemaking are drowned by the loud music accompanying the soft-porn clip playing in the next room (and lower left frame) for the production company of which Alex is a part. The clip muffles the sounds of the liaison from the company, as Alex intends, and from Lauren, as he could not have intended. Lauren is confused, now having reason to hope that her suspicions were a paranoid delusion. The film clip suddenly stops, and Rose's moans of passion leap across two frames to Lauren's headphones. Alex muffles Rose quickly, so the casting crew in the next room will not hear them.

But it's too late for Lauren. Her face dissolves slowly into despair as she hears the lover she merely suspected propose the idea of marriage to Alex, saying sweetly, "I can't have babies with Lauren . . ." He demurs, and she soon hears Rose turn angrily to the question of the audition: "You can't just come in here and fuck me and then get out of it."

A soap opera, no doubt about it. One set in a format that renders vivid the process by which passions first coalesce out of obscurity and then sometimes metamorphose into something else. Lauren did not know how she would respond to confirmation of her suspicion. It takes the event itself, resonating with the layered, affectively imbued memories that it calls up, to generate the feeling of despair, and then to transduct it more slowly into burning rage. She doesn't retreat into herself, as Emma does in the upper right frame as she becomes resigned to Alex's inability to reform and decides to leave him. We merely perceive that an upheaval is under way in Lauren, not discerning exactly what it is, what new events will collude and collide with it, and where these conjunctions will carry her. She seems to be possessed by a similar sense of uncertainty.

Another passion added to an intertwined world of becomings. Sure, after the fact you and I might "explain" the whole process, or fit the story into a familiar narrative scheme. Quantitative explanation or deep, authoritative interpretation, the two options competing unevenly for hegemony in the human sciences. Each is relatively easy to do. "It is a revenge story," say. But "it is always possible to take the latest phase of renovation, define it by a concept, and say that the others contained a greater or less quantity of what the concept includes, that therefore they all led up to the renovation. But things assume this form only in retrospect: the changes were qualitative and not quantitative; they defied all anticipation."[15]

To say that the changes are qualitative means that diverse elements melt into each other to spawn something irreducible to a combination of disparate factors. Perhaps we can go a bit further and suggest that the altered assemblage mixes qualitative and quantitative elements in an ensemble entirely reducible to neither.

Lauren does eventually shoot Alex. But what is a revenge story? Would it, moreover, have become a revenge story without the tremors? Besides, others in this story experience both the tremors and severe disappointments, and respond differently. And what or whom is Lauren's revenge enacted against? Against Alex, whom Lauren does not know? Against the world, for placing her in this mess? Or her own past as it is inserted into the present? These last two objects require stretching of the ready-made concept of revenge. Yes, the stylized concepts into which we regularly enclose such stories are relevant to life. But they do not entirely capture its flow as it unfolds. We could not deploy these capacious concepts before the event to anticipate exactly what happens. After the fact, we enclose a wide range of events in diffuse, ready-to-hand concepts, treating them as if they fit them like a body suit. Sure, we've seen a lot of revenge stories, and many of us don't really need another. But "things assume this form only in retrospect." And in retrospect you are on the edge of losing touch with the experience of duration, even while Life itself continues to unfold through it.

But, if, yet, however, besides, and, then, moreover, instead, perhaps, nevertheless . . . The connectives that populate our language may deserve more attention. They may suggest an awareness inside language of twists and swerves in the flow of time that all too readily get abstracted out when things are viewed retrospectively. The unfolding of events in each frame is punctuated by turns and surprises; these are periodically augmented, blocked, or reversed by words, sounds, entrances, gestures, calls, and shots arriving from outside the frame; those connections and disconnections, in turn, are amplified, ruptured, or intensified by music flowing to the audience and by a series of tremors shaking the very ground upon which the participants move. Out of these collisions surprising events, dissolutions, and consolidations appear. No single agent in this four-cornered world could predict how they would unfold. No single viewer can stay on top of every relevant development either, as the creative evolution unfolds—though many are tempted after the event to evaluate the "moral of the story" as if it unfolded according to an implacable logic that they endorse or, more likely, find to be bankrupt.

The inability to master the turns as they unfold arises only partly because the viewer and listener cannot attend closely to all frames at the same time. It also arises because each character dips into nonchronologically ordered waves of virtual memory that melt into experience and action below the level of attentiveness, combining in unexpected ways with events and pressures from adjacent frames.

Who could explain this mixing, remixing, and unmixing of multiple experiences? What about the tremors arriving at capricious times? Their preparation is set on a longer tier of chrono-time, breaking into the lived time of the participants at odd "moments." We have thus entered the territory of what might be called *emergent causation*, a mode of temporal flow irreducible to the efficient causality of social science or the webs of interdefinition so dear to narrative theory. Social scientists often separate elements closely interwoven and then strive to recombine them; devotees of interpretation often subtract fugitive *energies* that flow over, under, and through an established context, periodically infusing the complex with something new. Even the banal has an incredible complexity when it is in motion.

The mixing and remixing of open trajectories in *Time Code* may still fall short of the complexity of time in politics. You move a step closer to this complexity in *The Man Who Fell to Earth*. Here the savior who has fallen observes a panel of twelve TV screens simultaneously, performing a suprahuman structural analysis of cowboy films, talk shows, love stories, sitcoms, soap operas, sports events, and news broadcasts to make sense of American culture. He is invested with sensitivities we lack, such as the ability to engage in rapid parallel processing of disparate events at the conscious level. *Time Code* might be a breeze for him. We can only proceed slowly and serially at the conscious level, while participating in a bit of parallel processing at the nonconscious level. He can also hear the sounds and feel the pains accompanying past Indian wars as he walks across a barren piece of Texas desert. His map of Texas is four-dimensional. We cannot master the complexity of *Time Code* in one viewing, while he, with his impressive powers, still remains stumped by some developments on earth. Some of our feelings are alien to him.

The flow of duration is alteration in perdurance. We can usually endure it; we can often intervene in it; and we can periodically make this or that flow seem intelligible in retrospect. But we can't know it, master it, or draw it into a linear trajectory rolling along without twists, turns, or backflows, because of limits in our capacities as actors in the world, the involuted course of the world, and the dissonant conjunctions between them. Duration is time as becoming.

At this point the question can be posed, How can you even say that becoming is open if you do not have an image of a straight trajectory against which to make that determination? A fair question. The first thing to see is that the same question applies to every conception of time. How could you decide that time is linear unless you already knew the trajectory it was on? Or how do you determine that it follows an intrinsic purpose pulling it along? The answer in each case is bound to the human capacity of extrapolation. To say that time is becoming is to admit that at any moment we tend to project forward on the basis of preceding events and processes. The dictates of action-oriented perception and the pressures of clock time, as Bergson shows, support this prudential tendency. We project a path forward from the present. The difference between the trajectory projected and the variations or turns experienced provides a rough measure of continuity, twists, or turns in time. Often the line of continuity exceeds the pressure of variation. But sometimes a swerve disrupts a previous equilibrium, sending things off in a direction different enough from that extrapolated. The situation is similar to the question whether a trajectory generated by a simple set of rules is regular or random. The sense of what counts as either is bound to our previous experience of order. That experience may expand or mutate as our capacities and interests change. But at any given moment, it provides the rough measure of pattern or randomness, just as extrapolation from an existing equilibrium sets the measure against which we conclude that continuity exceeds variation or variation punctuates continuity. Duration is alteration within continuity.

Time and Ethico-Political Life

Conventional conceptions of meaning and causality are tied to an image of punctual time in which the past determines the future, rather than becoming real as the protraction of the present opens onto an underdetermined future recoiling back upon it. An extreme instance of the latter is trauma time, where an awful intrusion that unglues your very sense of trust in the world becomes an event susceptible to articulation (rather than merely painful flashbacks) only *after* it has been assigned a meaning and trajectory.[16] *It becomes what it was.* Our discussion of evil in chapter 1 can be understood through the back-to-front experience of trauma time. It is the back-to-front time that contending stories of evil try to capture, with limited success. Or consider the idea of involuntary memory advanced by Proust. As you encounter something that draws an earlier moment to the edge of awareness, a series of reverberations between the two moments foments an event irreducible to either alone. The reverberations spawn something new. Here is how Proust presents it:

> A moment of the past did I say? Was it not perhaps very much more: something that, common to both the past and to the present, is much more essential than either of them? So often in the past, in the course of my life, reality had disappointed me because at the instant my senses perceived it my imagination . . . could not apply itself to it, in virtue of that ineluctable law which ordains that we can only imagine what is absent. And now, suddenly, the effect of this harsh law had been neutralized, temporarily annulled, by a marvelous experience of nature which had caused a sensation . . . , to be mirrored at one and the same time in the past, so that my imagination was permitted to savor it, and in the present, where the actual shock to my senses . . . had added to the dreams of the imagination the concept of "existence" which they usually lack, and through this subterfuge had made it possible for my being to secure, to isolate, to immobilize—for a moment brief as a flash of lightning—what normally it never apprehends: a fragment of time in the pure state.[17]

A superb visualization of the result of such reverberations appears in the opening scene of *Far from Heaven*, a recent film that repeats with variations another film (*All That Heaven Allows*) first screened in the 1950s. Those brilliant orange, red, brown, and yellow leaves shining on the ground in the opening scene crystallize a series of reverberations between first and second experiences. What emerges was neither simply there then nor simply here now. It is engendered by a series of resonances between past and present as they coexist in the perdurance of duration. Here imagination and projection are sewn into the fabric of perception, as they always are to some degree. Think, say, of how an old neighborhood looks to you after an absence of twenty years. Or seeing a brief scene in a family film recovered after many years, as you run into the room as a two-year-old with your hat askew, check out the adults briefly, and then scamper off to more interesting fare off screen. Both trauma time and nostalgic perception bring out, through accentuation, the reverberations always operative in duration. In doing so, they suggest that it is wise to move thought beyond the assumption that punctual time is literal time, even if, as we shall see, it is also wise to retain a place in life for the *artifice* of chrono-time. The recurrent, cold nightmares of trauma and the warm resonances of nostalgia are not the same. But together they expose a rift in the structure of the moment, in which the past becomes what it was during the protraction of the present even as it is not entirely exhausted by what it now becomes. The starkness of trauma and the warmth of nostalgia allow us to glimpse how the new emerges in time.

To find a way to join the artifice of punctual time to time as becoming and out of joint it is necessary to rethink the ideas of cause and meaning too. We will set them mostly to the side for now, however. We will focus here on the intersection between morality, politics, and time. The dominant image of morality is bound to a progressive image of time. Any attempt to complicate that image of morality eventually runs up against the objection that it contradicts the way we *must* think about time if we are to be moral beings, or more fundamentally, if morality is to make sense *as* morality.

Kant offers an influential version of that view. For him, the basic experience of morality flows from the "apodictic recognition" that morality takes the form of a universal law you are obligated to obey. Once you run simple tests to decide whether each possible law actually passes the test of self-consistency, you are obligated to obey the laws that emerge. But, to put the point briefly, for the laws to be obligatory, it must be possible to realize them; and for that condition to hold we must project the possibility of continual progress toward their attainment. To act morally it is thus *necessary* to project the subjective potential of long-term moral progress. For "ought" implies "can," and the obligation to be moral presupposes that it is possible to be so.

A series of interlocking musts. Here is what Kant says in *Religion Within the Limits of Reason Alone* about the moral obligation to project individual and historical progress toward holiness—that is, toward that impossible moment when the dictates of morality conform to both the state of the self and the condition of the world: "But the distance separating the good which we ought to effect in ourselves from the evil whence we advance is infinite, and the act itself of conforming our course of life to the holiness of the law is impossible of execution in any given time. Nevertheless, man's moral constitution ought to accord with this holiness. This constitution must therefore be found in his disposition . . . A change of heart such as this must be possible because duty requires it . . . According to our mode of estimation, therefore, conduct itself, as a continual and endless advance from a deficient to a better good, ever remains defective . . . But we may also think of this endless progress of our goodness toward conformity to the law . . . as being judged by Him who knows the heart as a completed whole."[18]

The "endless progress of our goodness toward conformity to the law." Kant struggles here to negotiate a tension between two of his own convictions: first, that as human beings "straddling" two worlds we never attain fully the morality we are obligated to enact; second, that a moral law must be possible to attain if it is to be obligatory. As I read him he mitigates but does not erase this tension by asserting that the dictates of morality require us to act *as if* history is morally progressive; but the embodied character of human being also means that the end-point can never be reached in history. This combination leads to the necessary subjective projection of historical progress without final culmination. The course of progress parallels the paradoxical relation between the tortoise and Achilles in Zeno's paradox. Achilles keeps drawing closer, but at every "point in time," though the gap is reduced, there is always another gap to negotiate. The gap, while always narrowing, is never erased. Achilles never wins. The very logic of morality makes it incumbent upon us to project the possibility of indefinite historical progress

toward moral fulfillment, says Kant. But because we are embodied beings straddling two worlds, not "holy" beings subsisting entirely in one,
we must admit that the gap will never be overcome, either by individuals
or by universal history.

The first "must" in the series of Kantian musts is the most fateful
one. That is the idea that we do and must recognize morality to take the
form of law in the first instance. If you challenge the necessity of that
must, as Epicurus, Lucretius, Spinoza, Hume, Nietzsche, Freud, Bergson, James, the Dalai Lama, and I do, the difficulties attached to the
relation between ethics and time are not erased. But they are now phra-
sed and negotiated differently. Let us pursue this relation within an
orientation in which morality is not understood in the first instance to be
derived from apodictic recognition of its lawlike form but rather taken *to
be inspired* in the first instance by a love of the world or attachment to the
complexity of being that infuses it. The difference between morality and
ethics, on this reading, is in the kind of source from which each claims to
receive its most fundamental impetus.[19] The affirmation of obligation,
according to the second image, is a secondary effect of an ethic of cultivation rather than the primary expression of apodictic recognition.

Bergson also distinguishes between two sources of morality, though
they do not correspond exactly to the distinction posed above. The first
source, he says, is morality experienced by participants in a particular
society as a set of fixed obligations they are expected to meet to others in
that society as already divided by rank, function, and responsibility. The
morality of obligation is what he calls "closed morality," already distinguishing it from the idea of universal obligation in Kantian theory with
which it enters into contestation. He finds obligation to be indispensable
to a modicum of solidarity in cultural life. But such an obligation is not,
for him, grounded in the combination of apodictic recognition and tests
of universal consistency, as in Kant. The only universal is the obligation
to have obligations. The source and content of obligation is social pressure as it is contracted into habit and disposition. The embedded customs of obligation are often interpreted retrospectively to be grounded in
the commands of a god, or immutable tradition, or a categorical imperative. Bergson, however, does not embrace such sources. To him, the
sense of obligation dips into the evolutionary reserve of instinct, which

has been diminished by human intelligence but not eliminated entirely. For this reason the content of obligation varies with the society in which it is given shape, while the feeling attached to it arises from that in us which is closest to other animals. Bergson thus reverses Kant. He recognizes a place for obligation but anchors it in social convention, parochial bluntness, and residual instinct rather than apodictic recognition, universality, and the unconditional.

Bergson doubts that the morality of obligation through social pressure can expand far enough to encompass humanity writ large. Three impediments are operative. First, the obligations we recognize initially are toward those within a particular society; those outside the conventions at issue also fall outside their protection. Second, there is no source of obligation capable of capturing the whole world, since the instinct in which it is anchored is empty of content until it is filled with particular social conventions. Third, the "closed morality" of social obligation, because it presupposes progressive time, is ill equipped to come to terms with the twists and swerves in time that periodically punctuate social life.

The second dimension of Bergsonian morality—or ethics, as I will put it—is not wrapped in the experience of command or transcendental obligation. It is, rather, inspirational in character and sensitive to changes of context. *It is thereby capable of becoming responsive to unexpected shifts and turns in the flow of time.* It is inspired above all by prophets, saints, and heroes who draw people into their orbit as they come to terms with new circumstances not well covered by the extant moral code. Great prophets, mystics, saints, and heroes take the lead here, inspiring by their energy, care, and devotion others to modify some aspect of the code in force. Buddha, Jesus, Socrates, Epicurus, Thoreau, Nietzsche, Gandhi, and the Dalai Lama, among others, have manifested such energies; often they transmit them by contagion to others. They proceed primarily by attraction and example applied to new circumstances, not by commands attached to eternal laws. "True mystics simply open their souls to the oncoming wave . . . That which they have allowed to flow into them is a stream flowing down and seeking through them to reach their fellow-men; the necessity to spread around them what they have received affects them like an onslaught of love. A love which each one of them stamps with his own personality. A love which is in each of them an entirely new emotion, capable of transposing human life into another tone. A love which thus causes each of them to be loved for himself, so that through him, and for him, other men will open their souls to the love of humanity."[20]

Many today will recoil upon hearing these words, as well they might. These words can be twisted and transposed into authoritarian and even fascist messages. But amid these dangers, Bergson is onto something. It is pertinent to recall how he insists that the "two sources" of morality should be honored together in their tension and interdependence. And an excellent case can be made that the most compelling ethical innovators in history resonate with Bergson's characterization of mystical experience. Some of them place a God at the base of an experience they call mystical; others locate a radiant gratitude for being on the lower registers of human life. Place these two orientations side by side, and Plato, Augustine, Rousseau, Spinoza, Thoreau, Nietzsche, James, Hannah Arendt, Gilles Deleuze, and Charles Taylor can be said to tap into one or the other. You find variants of it not only in the *caritas* of Augustine, love of the world in Arendt, and gratitude for the abundance of being amid suffering in Nietzsche: it even finds muted expression in Kantian moral theory. Sure, Kant distinguishes sharply between sensuous feeling and the practical reason that rises above it. But as he addresses the question of how the self comes to *recognize* and *feel* obligated to obey the moral law, he is compelled to articulate a feeling of respect for morality that is "nonsensuous" and "nonpathological" in origin. This nonsensuous impetus, in contrast to the sensuous feelings and inclinations it must often override, "lies in pure practical reason; because of its origin, therefore, this particular feeling cannot be said to be pathologically effected . . . ; it lessens the obstacle to pure practical reason and produces the idea of the superiority of its objective law to the impulses of sensuousness."[21]

Kantian respect is, in Bergson's words, "an emotion capable of transposing life into another tone." Kant, of course, closely hedges in the impetus that respect provides, so that it can generate an impetus to action but not be free to roam as widely as comparable energies do in Bergson, James, and Nietzsche. Indeed, one tricky problem confronting Kant is how to explain why the practical reason he takes to be universal does not really arrive in history until after he has elaborated the theory that expresses it. Kant insists that we must take this nonsensuous feeling of respect to be supersensuous in origin and expression, while James and Bergson discern it to flow into human sensibility itself from a diffuse higher realm. These differences pose fundamental issues, as does the Nietzschean idea that the aura of generosity accompanying gratitude for being is earthy all the way down. But the point to focus on now is that every convincing ethical philosophy makes room *somewhere* for the impetus of what Bergson calls mystical experience, Kant calls the nonsensuous feeling of respect, and Nietzsche calls earthy gratitude for the abundance of being. The differences are very important, but the impetus to ethical action would disappear if you dropped out this aspect, as contemporary neo-Kantians sometimes do out of fear of succumbing to authoritarian drives, or lapsing into an ethic without the guidance of universal criteria, or caving in to the authority of a religion of the Book.

Bergson joins James in thinking that something akin to mystical experience moves and shapes those transfigurations of thought-imbued affect that enable new modes of receptivity and generosity to come into being. Such a shift finds its highest expression in a "bent for action, the faculty of adapting and re-adapting oneself to circumstances, in firmness combined with suppleness, in the prophetic discernment of what is possible and what is not."[22] Most of us experience echoes of such states, even if, as in my case, they are not as vivid as those that James and Bergson report. James and Bergson attach these experiences to the soft whisper of transcendence. But it is important to see how others, emphasizing them just as strongly, link them to infrasensible sources that do not take the shape of a personal divinity. Buddha, the Dalai Lama, Spinoza, and Nietzsche may all provide diverse examples.

Take creativity in thinking, for instance. Suppose that the experience of ethics you have imbibed to this point is tied to a progressive image of time that both enables and fetters it. You have rethought received views of ethics to some degree, but you are tied to the progressive image of time in which the dominant model of morality is set. You sense diffusely that something is amiss, but you do not have a well-defined sense of the issue. Nonetheless, vague, affectively imbued thoughts somehow associated with it well up from time to time. Until one day, as if from nowhere, you are flooded with a protean feeling that an undernoted dimension in your own experience of time holds a key to help you rethink ethical life. Such a thought, bubbling to the surface with intense energy, resonates with the Bergsonian idea of mystical experience, while not necessarily being fettered to the idea of a limited divinity in which Bergson invests it. After that experience, there is a lot of work to do. But you do not now merely have a dim sense of how to proceed, you are also flooded with *energy* to pursue the project. The result, once the relevant issues are engaged, may not turn out as projected during this minor epiphany. You may have to return to the drawing board, or even be compelled to drop a thought that once seemed promising. But sometimes the premonition turns out to be key. And it becomes clear once again how dry and sterile the adventure of thought would be if you did not periodically first experience the upheaval of a new premonition and then pursue it to the hilt until it is either set aside or preserved through modifications. You proceed by dwelling in a previously obscure experience of duration, proceeding with "firmness combined with suppleness, in . . . discernment of what is possible and what is not" in a world that moves faster than it did when Augustine and Kant bound morality and progressive time tightly together.

It is therefore how you express and modulate this dimension of thinking and ethics that is critical, not how to eliminate it. It is in the dissonant conjunction between new swerves of time and the ethical uncertainty they engender that it becomes imperative to "transpose human life into another tone." These are often dangerous moments, but they may also be recurrent and ineliminable. If Buddha, Socrates, and Jesus imparted new energies to the world at critical forks in time, it seems likely that the world will again stand in need of new infusions as new forks arrive.

Bergson, raised by one Christian and one Jewish parent, composed much of his philosophy before the Second World War and the consolidation of totalitarianism. He died after he contracted pneumonia while waiting in line in Paris to register as a Jew during the Nazi occupation. Instead of continuing to cull kernels from his work while extracting dangers and worries he did not always anticipate, I now turn to ethicopolitical virtues appropriate to a pluralist culture in a world marked by forks and turns in time.

The Politics of Becoming

By the politics of becoming I mean that paradoxical politics by which new and unforeseen things surge into being, such as a new and surprising religious faith, a new source of moral inspiration, a new mode of civilizational warfare, a new cultural identity unsettling an existing constellation of established identities, a new collective good, or the placement of a new right on the existing register of recognized rights. In highlighting the importance of becoming to politics, I do not disparage the importance of being, though I have learned through experience that some who focus only on being find it difficult to absorb a theory in which becoming and being are maintained in a relation of torsion. They focus only on the discussion of becoming, forgetting the appreciation of being against which it is balanced.

In my vocabulary the politics of being refers to crystallizations that persist, even as subterranean forces may accumulate within them. The politics of being provides indispensable points of reference for politics, judgment, and action. But there are times when the politics of becoming in a given zone accelerates. Today, for instance, it is arguable that the suicide bomber changes the established contours of international politics, as the bombers fight for a vision of civilization by means exceeding traditional revolutionary organization, national insurgency, and state military machines. On another, more promising front there is the drive to place the right of doctor-assisted suicide on the register of recognized rights. Forty years ago that claim was not even simmering as a minority report among moralists who defined themselves as defenders of the definitive list of human rights. The new demand is not *derived* from a thick set of principles containing it implicitly all along. If it eventually acquires a sedimented place in the order of things, it will be *pressed* and *negotiated* into being by an assemblage of insurgents who demand it and respondents who combine attention to new medical technologies and sensitivity to human suffering, aided by the fatigue of erstwhile opponents.

The politics of becoming does not always generate positive things. Far from it. But it emerges out of historically specific suffering, previously untapped energies, and emerging lines of possibility eluding the attention of dominant constituencies. In successful instances the politics of becoming moves from a netherworld below the register of positive acceptance, identity, legitimacy, or justice onto one or more of those registers. To cross that threshold is to shake up something in the established world. It is to propel a fork in political time, throwing a wrench into the established code of obligation, goodness, identity, justice, right, or legitimacy.

The *politics* of becoming, again, is not the only way in which forks in time arise. Biological and climatic evolution, for instance, provide other exemplifications. These modes of becoming, moreover, periodically converge or collide with movements in the politics of becoming. The intensive human use of fossil fuels, for instance, may collide or collude with shifts in climatic development already under way. Or an emergent virus may fall into the hands of terrorists. In the contemporary world, when the tempo of life has accelerated in several domains, the politics of becoming is more active, widespread, and visible than heretofore. This era is one in which many ethico-political conflicts take the form of one set of drives to open up avenues of pluralization and another to return to a slower time when a more homogeneous image of time was easier to sustain. Two paths of becoming in conflict, each spurred by the acceleration of pace in the fastest zones of modern life, each intensified by the other, each seeking to alter the flow of time, and each too, perhaps, inspired by a different image of time.

What political virtues are most appropriate to a contemporary world in which the politics of becoming has accelerated, interdependent constituencies honor different final moral sources, and the interdependent partisans do not have recourse to authoritative arguments sufficient to dissolve all their differences in a sea of commonality? What civic virtues, more closely, are appropriate to those committed to pluralism? The virtues commended here do not take politics out of ethics, nor do they rise above politics. *Rather, they lend an ethical dimension to the experience of identity, the practice of faith, the promotion of self-interest, and the engagements of politics.* They speak to a world in which people draw upon different final sources of ethical sustenance and bring those sources with them into politics. I note two such civic virtues.

The first is agonistic respect. It is a relation between interdependent partisans who have already attained a place on the register of cultural recognition—that is, on the register of being. Agonistic respect is a kissing cousin of liberal tolerance. But liberal tolerance is bestowed upon private minorities by a putative majority occupying the authoritative, public center. You may have noticed that people seldom enjoy being tolerated that much, since it carries the onus of being at the mercy of a putative majority that often construes its own position to be beyond question.

In a political ethos of agonistic respect between multiple constituencies honoring different final faiths, however, the public center becomes more finely sliced and diffuse. The interdependent partisans do not automatically leave the different creeds or final ethical sources to which they appeal in the private realm. So the respect side of the relationship comes from different sources for different constituencies. The respect between them is deep precisely to the extent that each can respect the other in drawing its respect from a source unfamiliar to it. Several, of course, may leave large pieces and chunks of their faith in the closet, to the extent that the issue at hand makes it feasible to do so. That is one way to express relational modesty about the faith you honor. When the issue in question makes it necessary to bring aspects of their basic faith-philosophy into the public realm, the partisans adopt a certain forbearance and hesitancy with respect to its practical universalizability, out of respect for the relative opacity of their faith to others and in acknowledgment of their own inability, to date, to demonstrate its truth. In a relation of agonistic respect, partisans may test, challenge, and contest pertinent elements in the fundaments of the others. But each also appreciates the comparative contestability of its own fundaments to others, drawing upon this bicameralism of citizenship to inform their negotiations.

An ethos of agonistic respect grows out of mutual appreciation for the ubiquity of faith to life and the inability of contending parties, to date, to demonstrate the truth of one faith over other live candidates. It grows out of reciprocal appreciation for the element of contestability in these domains. The relation is agonistic in two senses: you *absorb the agony* of having elements of your own faith called into question by others, and you *fold agonistic contestation* of others into the respect that you convey toward them.

The participants are apt to share some understandings about obligations and rights. They do participate in the politics of being. But in a fast-paced world, the sedimented code of obligation periodically proves insufficient to new public settlements. The feeling of obligation, as Bergson notes, is applied most ardently to those who share religious, linguistic, and moral traditions with you. It runs into its limits in a culture of deep pluralism. In such a world it is important to negotiate oblique *connections* across multiple lines of difference, negotiating agonistic respect between constituencies who embrace different final faiths and do not comprehend each other all that well.

But how could such a connection be forged, without falling into disconnected individualism, devolving into substantive commonality, or dissolving entirely into a set of common procedures? Here is one example. Sometimes the diastolic rhythm of one constituency resonates strangely with the systolic beat of others. Here a seed of oblique *connection* emerges between partisans honoring different creeds. Thus Epicurus, a functional nontheist, advised his disciples to subdue worry about what happens *after* death in order to overcome that resentment of human mortality that lends a punitive cast to morality. He thus acknowledged, before the advent of Christianity, how a subterranean flow of faith in an afterlife readily infiltrates the subliminal lives of those who officially eschew it. Several monotheists, including Kierkegaard, James, and Bergson, testify to similar dissonances, though they locate them in the forgetfulness that periodically punctuates faith in transcendence. What if many on each side of such a divide can identify a little atheist or theist periodically peeking through their dominant investments of faith? What if they then pursue connections across such chiasmatic lines? Attention to such a connection can provoke laughter . . . as each constituency engages an internal *counterpoint* to itself that tempers the *external counterpart* it provides to others.

This laughter, bubbling up as if from nowhere, bursts into being from a fund of abundance below consciousness.[23] As it surges forth, it may signify how contestable the mystical interpretation of becoming is to those who participate in an experience that resonates with it but does not coincide with it. And vice versa. It does not require refined intellectuality to laugh together on these occasions.

This is a juncture at which (to confine ourselves to perspectives already mentioned) self-modest Buddhists, Kantians, Augustinians, Jamesians, Bergsonites, and Nietzscheans might meet. They do not connect through thick *agreement* upon a common source of justice, obligation, philosophy, or creed. Nor are common procedures *sufficient* to them. On top of these points of overlap and difference they connect positively through reciprocal confession that those in each group confront doubts, forgetfulness, or uncertainties in themselves that may invert those confronted by others. When such crossings are explored without resentment, they can evolve into reciprocal commitment to inject generosity and forbearance into public negotiations between parties who reciprocally acknowledge that the deepest wellsprings of human inspiration are to date susceptible to multiple interpretations. They evolve toward a public ethos of agonistic respect rather than devolving entirely into the public tolerance of private differences.

Such a connection is inspired by mutual appreciation of the human inability to dissolve operational differences about final ethical sources into a public matrix of consensus. The *respect* may now expand as each constituency solicits with new vigor sources of relational generosity within its own faith. The *pain of agonism* against which respect is balanced expresses reciprocal appreciation of how carriers of another creed may press you to sharpen or modify yours, in response to distinctive questions, examples, and sensitivities. In a relation of agonistic respect, something in the faith, identity, or philosophy of the engaged parties is placed at risk. On occasion, these interdependent contenders may be compelled by events to band together more adamantly, as they struggle to limit intransigent unitarians who insist that the final source *they* confess must be professed or obeyed by everyone.

Agonistic respect is a cardinal virtue of deep pluralism. It applies to circumstances in which the forking of time has already crystallized into interdependent constituencies divided by multiple differences of faith, income, sensibility, household arrangement, sensual affiliation, and gender practice. A second virtue, irreducible to agonistic respect, is critical responsiveness. It is appropriate to the politics of becoming *while it is still under way*. It is thus a civic virtue particularly pertinent to a time when the fastest zones of life move at a more rapid tempo than heretofore, the politics of becoming proceeds on several fronts, and citizen action periodically reaches above state boundaries as well as operating within them.

Critical responsiveness takes the form of *careful listening and presumptive generosity* to constituencies struggling to move from an obscure or degraded subsistence below the field of recognition, justice, obligation, rights, or legitimacy to a place on one or more of those registers. When a place is created new terms of contrast and similarity become available and the entire register is altered to some degree. When the politics of becoming surges in one domain or another, inspiration and a suppleness of mind are needed to adjust old codes of interest, obligation, and principle to new and surprising events. It is not that the participants "lack" standards of judgment. Such standards are plentiful. *It is that some of those very standards now constitute part of the problem.* Creative thinking is needed to decide which standards to recompose and which to draw upon to inform the recomposition.

Agonistic respect and critical responsiveness are civic virtues that require both internal constituency cultivation and public negotiation. They emerge at the points of intersection between individual work and micropolitics. They involve tactical work on that affective register of being which flows into the higher intellect but is not highly amenable to direct regulation by it. Attention to the layering of affect thereby points to another way in which neither virtue is reducible to the most familiar liberal virtues. For liberal virtues are often defined as if they find full expression on the highest intellectual register, as if repetition, image processing, and ritual performance are not important to their very composition and maintenance. The cultivation of critical responsiveness, however, involves considerable work on the visceral register of the responding constituency. To cultivate critical responsiveness to a new movement in the politics of becoming is at once to work tactically on gut feelings already sedimented into you, to readdress refined concepts previously brought to these issues, and to work on the circuits through which the former connect to the latter. The civic virtue of critical responsiveness taps that well of creative receptivity that Bergson, James, Nietzsche, and the Dalai Lama, in different ways, find so critical to ethico-political life.

Suppose you find it incumbent to modify some aspect of the visceral sensibility that has grown up in you like tropical underbrush. Perhaps you had taken your own sexual desire to monopolize the natural field. Or had felt instinctively that your religious creed, so radiant to you, is binding on everyone. Your initial response to a new movement in the domain of creed or sexuality may be to attack it as unnatural, to protect the security of your visceral identity. How could people screw like that?, you ask, feeling tremors of uncertainty course through your own sexual identity. How could an existential *faith* be nontheistic?, you ask, resisting the creation of any space in between monotheistic faith and rationalistic orientations that purport to eschew faith altogether. But another voice in you worries about the indignity or suffering imposed on others by such patterns of insistence. Now the cultivation of critical responsiveness begins.[24] It proceeds in conjunction with exposure to a larger micropolitics. The outcome is uncertain. But it may alter part of the context in which judgments are formed and negotiations are pursued. It may engender a shift in criteria of judgment, justice, identity, or legitimacy.

Critical responsiveness is *critical* in that it does not always accede to everything that a new constituency or movement demands. But the catch is this: The criticism is not securely guided by established codes or criteria of interpretive judgment. For some of them turn out to be part of the problem. This is the crucial moment to tap an open reserve of receptivity not entirely captured by the ethico-political criteria of judgment heretofore absorbed. For when selective elements in the existing context of judgment are thrown into doubt by an unexpected turn in time, suppleness is needed. Cultivation of creativity, close attunement to new circumstances, preliminary receptivity to negotiation, and a readiness to explore how some element in received standards might be in need of selective recomposition—these are subvirtues simmering within the practice of critical responsiveness.

The Double Coding of Time

At this point the following charge might be issued:

"But in posing this connection between time and ethics don't you, at a second level, reinstate the relation between ethics and progressive time? For you seem to be saying that ethical progress is made as agonistic respect and critical responsiveness become integrated more actively into the ethos of deep pluralism. Isn't it time, Connolly, to reassert the relation between morality and a progressive image of time?"

The charge of the "performative contradiction" rears its head. My sense, indeed, is that the widespread academic commitment to what James and Bergson call "intellectualism" in the human sciences is attractive to many partly because its tightly ordered images of concept, cause, and cultural logic allow theorists to make the performative contradiction the master tool of critical theory. Once you adopt a more layered image of culture and a philosophy of time as becoming, however, the charge loses some of its bite. The dense materiality of culture does not correspond to such a tightly ordered logic. But still, what is my response to the charge?

Well, I grant something in the point, while taking a different perspective on the issue. I have not claimed that we should scotch the punctual and progressive images of time. Far from it. In everyday, action-oriented perception we do project such images, and it is prudential to do so. This is precisely what Bergson himself concludes in his exploration of perception. Moreover, as we project desirable possibilities and responsibilities forward in situations in which established interpretations of goodness, justice, and legitimacy are working reasonably well, we do link the exercise of responsibility to the possibility of progress in a single direction. And it is wise to do so.

But that is only part of the story. What about those protean moments when we are hit by surprising events and movements that throw aspects of our previous projections into disarray? These are precisely the moments, first, when the experience of time as becoming becomes most poignant and, second, when the public virtue of critical responsiveness becomes most crucial to pluralist politics. So, as I suggested at the outset, I do not seek to *replace* a punctual image of time with time as creative evolution. I seek, rather, to complicate the experience of time, drawing upon each modality at different moments. The first is the image of time through which everyday perception is organized, reinforced by the disciplines of clock time through which much of modern life is coordinated: the politics of being. The second is the experience of time out of joint as we dwell in duration to focus on the politics of becoming.

Today, when the world spins faster than heretofore, *it has become wise to adopt a double-entry orientation to the experience of political time.* When things are relatively sedate in some zone or other—that is, when there is the relative arrest that I call the politics of being—you pursue the codes of justice, legitimacy, and obligation with which you have been imbued, projecting the possibility of progress forward from that point. As the politics of becoming escalates in a particular zone of life, however, you dwell again in that uncanny experience in which time is out of joint, in which past and present resonate back and forth in the contingency of an unexpected encounter. Now you seek to activate sensitivities appropriate to an unfolding situation, acknowledging the extent to which a rapid shift in events has thrown into doubt some dimension in the undergrowth which gives density and specificity to established principles. You don't toss your principles aside. You strive to become more supple and sensitive about the tension between new experience and the underbrush of prejudgments heretofore attached to them.

If, after that, a new settlement is consolidated in the code of justice or goodness, you may again project the possibility of ethical progress forward from that point. Hence, a double-entry orientation to time, encouraged by the complexity of ethico-political life.

Yes, if we fold a double-entry orientation to time into the practice of ethics, it can be said that we have made ethical progress. But unless one has a prior commitment to a Hegelian reading of *Geist*, a bit of a paradox now clings to that formulation. If that bit is forgotten, things readily lapse back into the dogmatism of the single-entry, punctual view contested here as insufficient to politics. The touch of paradox is that on my reading, a double-entry orientation to the experience of time must be widely adopted to make it possible to say that ethical progress is being made. To embrace *that* duplicity is to move a distance from, say, Augustine and Kant on the relation between faith, morality, and time. What you take from them is the idea that you do tend to project forward from each consolidated interpretation of responsibility to the future. What you subtract from them is the obligation to act *as if* you already know the shape that those dense principles, rights, obligations, and legitimate identities must assume in the future.

To adopt a double-entry orientation to the conjunctions between politics, ethics, and time is to open yourself on occasion to new breezes blowing softly through the subterranean tissues of life, sometimes enabling a creative evolution in ethico-political life to meet the arrival of new circumstances. It is a big step to consider a change in the dominant image of time. But such a step is no bigger today than, say, the earlier one from the cosmic view of purposive causality that we now call finalism to the coarse idea of efficient causality set in a linear pattern of change. That is, it is a big step but, perhaps, a possible and worthy one. To embrace a double-entry orientation to time in this way is to acknowledge the fragility of deep pluralism and the recurrent need for ethical suppleness on the part of those attentive to its fragility.

CHAPTER 5

PLURALISM AND
SOVEREIGNTY

The Gang of Five

I am an American who votes Democratic. I note this unsurprising fact to mark a defining feature of politics in a democratic state. Democratic politics requires partisanship. Does it also depend upon access to an impartial standard, procedure, or constitution through which to regulate partisanship? The answer is complex. The public authority of democratic constitutionalism cannot be established by fidelity to a written text alone. It cannot because, first, a constitution consists of words whose meanings are not definitively fixed even when initially composed; second, those words must later be applied in new and unforeseen circumstances; and third, the spirit through which the open-textured document is applied must give priority to public elections if the democratic element of constitutionalism is to be honored. If judicial authorities in a demo-constitutional state override this last consideration, citizens' trust in the wisdom of judicial decisions becomes corroded.

Knowing this much, you will not be surprised to learn how outraged

I was over the handling of the recount issues during the presidential election of 2000. The key participants were the Republican secretary of state of Florida, the Republican governor, the Republican state legislature, the national Republican campaign, the hired Republican guns who intimidated the recount commission in one district at a pivotal moment, and above all the Gang of Five Republican-appointed judges on the Supreme Court, who stopped the vote-counting process before Bush's razor-thin lead would have been subjected to a recount of disputed ballots. I did not expect the parties to rise above partisanship, in the sense of applying a neutral standard wholly independent of it. I doubt there is such a place to which to rise. I expected the majority of the Supreme Court to fold partisanship for the integrity of democratic elections into its interpretation of the porous words of the law and Constitution, using those considerations to chasten partisanship for the candidate it favored. In this instance, however, the Gang of Five first jumped headlong into a situation they could have avoided or entered hesitantly and then halted the vote count authoritatively. They allowed partisan loyalty to a candidate to override partisanship for democracy in a setting where the applicable principles provided ample possibility to go in the other direction. That partisanship reduced public confidence in the Court and eroded the bonds of trust between partisans upon which the legitimacy of a democratic state depends.

Most of the Gang of Five present themselves as "strict constructionists." That allows them to pretend that no partisanship is involved in their decisions. But the doctrine of strict constructionism received a body blow from this action. Citizens who had ignored esoteric debates over the logic of constitutional interpretation now saw that doctrine and this decision placed side by side. The cover of strict constructionism was blown. That was mostly to the good. But because strict constructionism retains a prominent presence in popular discourse about constitutional interpretation, the loss of belief that the Court is guided by it exacerbates public cynicism.

In the middle of this quagmire, Justice Souter, previously appointed by a Republican president, emerges as a hero. Here are some statements from his dissenting opinion:

If this court had allowed the state to follow the course indicated by the opinions of its own Supreme Court, it is entirely possible that there would ultimately have been no issue requiring our review.

None of the state court interpretations were unreasonable to the point of displacing the legislative enactment quoted. As I will note below, other interpretations were of course possible and some might have been better than those adopted by the Florida court's majority . . .

The [state legislature's] statute does not define a "legal vote" . . . The State Supreme Court was therefore required to define it, and in doing that the court looked to another election statute . . . which contains a provision that no vote may be disregarded "if there is a clear indication of the intent of the voter as determined by a canvassing board."

The majority might have concluded that "rejection" should refer to machine malfunction . . . There is, however, nothing nonjudicial in the Florida majority's more hospitable reading . . . Whatever people of good will and good sense may argue about the merits of the Florida Court's reading, there is no warrant for saying that it transcends the limits of reasonable statutory interpretation.[1]

Justice Souter acknowledges that the judges found themselves in uncharted territory. His language of "good will," "good sense," and "reasonable statutory interpretation" conveys the sensibility that he brings to such recurrent moments. He also expresses presumptive partiality for democracy when he seeks to allow "the state the opportunity to count all disputed ballots now." When Souter encounters uncertainty in electoral law he fills it with a partisanship in favor of counting the votes of all citizens.

What does this event teach about the challenge of sovereignty in a democratic state? What, more closely, is the relation between sovereignty and law at such moments of uncertainty? What kind of sensibility on the part of judges and ethos on the part of citizens is pertinent to democratic pluralism?

The Ethos of Sovereignty

According to theorists from a variety of intellectual traditions, the Florida election case reflects a fundamental paradox located at the center of the rule of law in a democratic society. Jean-Jacques Rousseau, Carl Schmitt, Franz Kafka, Paul Ricoeur, Hannah Arendt, Bonnie Honig, Jacques Derrida, Alan Keenan, Gilles Deleuze, Giorgio Agamben, Michael Hardt, and Antonio Negri, while disagreeing on numerous issues, concur in asserting that a democratic state seeking to honor the rule of law is also one in which a sovereign power operating both inside and outside the law is brought into play. Since the paradox expresses the lawlessness upon which the rule of law depends it is often hidden from public view. Strict constructionism is merely one doctrine by which this rift at the center of constitutionalism is obscured.

While all these theorists confront the paradox of sovereignty, only a few link it to the politics of becoming. But the two are intimately connected. Because of the politics of becoming, gaps and fissures open up periodically between positional sovereignty as the highest authority to interpret the law and sovereignty as the effective power to decide what it will be. These two dimensions of sovereignty often shade into one another. But the discrepancy sometimes becomes a fissure that is too dramatic to ignore.

Rousseau, the key founder of democratic theory, concentrates the paradox in the founding of a republic, asserting that "for an emerging people to appreciate healthy maxims . . . and follow the fundamental rules of statecraft, the effect would have to become the cause."[2]

That is, for a government of self-rule to come into being out of a nondemocratic condition, the public ethos needed for democratic governance would have to be preceded by the kind of laws that nourish it; but those good laws, in turn, would need to be preceded by that very ethos if *they* were to emerge. The laws and the ethos must precede each other. That is the paradox of founding. Rousseau resolved it through recourse to the fiction of a wise Legislator above the law who imbues people with an ethos of self-rule. He knew that this fiction was insufficient to the actuality of any people filled with undemocratic customs, priorities, habits, and norms. He knew, in other words, that it is exceedingly difficult to found a democracy in a place that is not already democratic. Moreover, he knew that words, rules, and laws encounter uncertainty as they bump into new and unforeseen circumstances.[3] He thus saw that even when a democracy is successfully founded, the paradox returns as a recurring dimension of democratic sovereignty.

His response is to imagine a regime where time crawls slowly, so that a homogeneous ethos of sovereignty can persist across generations. He also endorses an extensive micropolitics to install in the populace the very sentiments they are supposed to will into being through autonomous acts of governing. He thus supports a simple, single, public faith; a unified educational system; yearly festivals and rituals in which all citizens participate; close regulation of the theater; a common mode of dress for adults to discourage amorous relations with foreigners; tight rules of chastity to curtail the passions; a nuclear family that the adult male alone represents in public life; the minimization of commerce inside the regime and its further reduction with merchants outside; a society of self-subsistent farms; severe restrictions on economic inequality; a citizen militia in which all young adult males serve; and so on and on. The effect of these institutions, disciplines, prohibitions, and channels is to install the same habits, sentiments, and self-restraints in the citizenry, to create a national ethos of sovereignty.

Rousseau could have provided a good critique of strict constructionism. He might have said that while it is represented as providing the means by which to give detached readings of the constitution, those readings actually express a conjunction between the text and mores that permeate the sensibilities of judges and citizens. Put another way, strict constructionism juridicalizes the ruse that Rousseau invested in the legislator whom he introduced to negotiate the paradox of democratic founding. "It is this sublime reason, which rises above the grasp of common men, whose decisions the legislator places in the mouths of the immortals in order to convince by divine authority those who cannot be moved by human prudence."[4] Substitute the phrase "the judges place into the mouths of the founding fathers" for "the legislator places in the mouths of the immortals" and you uncover the esoteric meaning of strict constructionism. Strict constructionism is a political formula that bathes the discretionary power of judges in the rhetoric of servitude to an abstract document.

No democrat has plumbed the paradox of democratic sovereignty more deeply than Rousseau. But for all that, the ethos he supports is too far out of touch with defining features of contemporary life to pass muster today. His response demands a small, isolated, unitarian polity crawling along at a snail's pace, while we inhabit large, pluralistic states, tied to global networks of power, in which the gap between the fastest and slowest zones of culture is large. Rousseau does not negotiate a response through which democracy, pluralism, law, and sovereignty speak affirmatively to each other in a fast-paced world. For that very reason, however, he does help us to discern why the desire to return to a slow world so easily becomes hitched to the micropolitics of strict constructionism and democratic fundamentalism.

Biopolitics and Micropolitics

Giorgio Agamben contends that the paradox of sovereignty has become stark in late modernity as the state has installed itself deeply into biological life. Biological issues become prominent in state decisions regarding abortion, artificial insemination, the line between life and death, organ transplants, the treatment of prisoners of war, social disciplines, strategies of citizen induction, and policies of "racial" inclusion and exclusion.

The democratic state, Agamben says, requires a final authority to resolve questions of law, while that authority must often exceed the law in making its decisions. Modern sovereignty carries forward, if implicitly, the pagan logic of *homo sacer*, or the sacred man. Homo Sacer is "the life that cannot be sacrificed and yet may be killed."[5] This state logic is connected to sovereignty because the "sovereign sphere is the sphere in which it is permitted to kill without committing homicide and without celebrating a sacrifice."[6] The "logic" that binds sovereignty, the sacred, and biopolitics together, Agamben contends, leads to a state in which a supreme power can annihilate an entire minority in the name of national unity. It is the nexus between sovereignty, the sacred, and biopolitics that makes the concentration camp the paradigm of modern politics, with the Nazi regime expressing its outer limit. When you add the Guantánamo gulag and Abu Ghraib to the list it is apparent how Agamben extends the paradox of American sovereignty from a constitutional dispute over an election to the logic of imperial power.

Agamben finds the paradoxical logic of sovereignty so immovable that he seeks a way to overcome its aporias entirely. Here are two formulations announcing that necessity:

> And only if it is possible to think the relation between potentiality and actuality differently—and even to think beyond this relation—will it be possible to think a constituting power wholly released from the sovereign ban. Until [this happens] a political theory freed from the aporias of sovereignty remains unthinkable.
>
> Only if it is possible to think the Being of abandonment beyond every idea of law will we have moved out of the paradox of sovereignty toward a politics of freedom from every ban.[7]

Nowhere in the book, however, is a way out actually proposed. Agamben thus carries us through the conjunction of sovereignty, the sacred, and biopolitics to a historical impasse. Sovereignty is indispensable to modern politics but it generates an unacceptable result. Is it possible to slip through Agamben's insistence that the paradox must be overcome entirely by rethinking the logic of his analysis? I think so. I will suggest that while Agamben is insightful in identifying key elements in sovereignty and in pointing to their dangers, the very formalism of his analysis disarms the most promising route to negotiate these issues. I will examine three elements in his account: the role of the sacred, the relation between biopolitics and sovereignty, and the "logic" of sovereignty.

Something might be sacred because it is held to represent divinity, or be a book that is divinely inspired, or be a ruler divinely authorized, or be a set of rituals expressing the highest human relation to the divine. Those who disturb or snub such things are said to deserve punishment, or even death, not because they touch the sacred but because they do so in a blasphemous way. They translate a divine symbol into an idol; or mock a sacred text; or ridicule a beloved priesthood; or disparage a sacred constitution. Spinoza was cursed and banned because he challenged the faith of the Elders in the beleaguered Hebrew community of Amsterdam in the seventeenth century. The banning fits Agamben's model of one who is "included while being excluded." But Spinoza is counted as a pariah through exclusion because he defiled the sacred, not because he participated in it. When I call a governing faction of the Supreme Court the "Gang of Five," some will say that I show lack of awe for a body that occupies an essential role at the heart of sovereignty. To them, I defile a sacred institution.

There is often ambivalence in people's orientation to the sacred, an ambivalence concealed through fear of retribution by God or their compatriots. Those demanding punishment of others who defile what they take to be sacred, familiarly enough, often intensify the demand because of the very ambivalence that they themselves feel. Spinoza, Nietzsche, and Freud, among others, read the punishment of blasphemy in this way. And each himself was accused of blasphemy because of that very analysis. None, however, says that *homo sacer* is part of the sacred.

The issue is pertinent because in a political culture of deep pluralism—a culture in which people honor different existential faiths and final sources of morality—different images of the sacred unavoidably and repeatedly bump into each other. What is needed today is a cautious relaxation of discourse about the sacred, one that allows us to come to terms affirmatively with the irreducible plurality of sacred objects in late modern life. With respect to sovereignty it is important to underline the significance of acts by which deep conflicts are settled; but it is equally important not to elevate them to the level of the sacred.

Agamben also contends that biopolitics has intensified today. That intensification translates the paradox of sovereignty into a potential disaster. It is well to recall, however, that every way of life involves the infusion of norms, judgments, and standards into the affective life of participants. Every way of life is bicultural and biopolitical. Lucretius, Augustine, Spinoza, Rousseau, and Merleau-Ponty, writing at different periods, all appreciate the layering of culture into biological life. They treat the biological not as merely the genetic or the fixed but also as the introjection of culture into interwired layers of corporeality.

The moment of truth in Agamben's account is that late modern life technologies deployed by physicians, biologists, geneticists, prisons, corporate advertisers, military training camps, televangelists, media talking heads, filmmakers, and psychiatrists do sink deeply into the grammar of human biology. They help to shape bicultural being. Agamben's review of new medical technologies to keep people breathing after their brains have stopped functioning signifies the importance of this change, showing how a sovereign authority now must decide when death has arrived rather than let such a decision reflect the slow play of biocultural forces. Numerous such judgments, previously left to religious tradition in predominantly Christian cultures, now become explicit issues of law and sovereignty in religiously diverse ones.

But Agamben also tends to describe the state as a "nation-state." He fails to ask whether the disturbing developments that he charts flow not simply from a conjunction between biopolitics and sovereignty but from a more fateful accord between them and intensive drives to national unitarianism. If the reactive drive to restore the fictive unity of a Christian—or even Judeo-Christian—nation is relaxed, it becomes possible to negotiate a more generous ethos in which sovereignty is practiced. The nexus between biology, politics, and sovereignty remains in a pluralist culture. But the most ominous dangers of sovereignty are reduced. Put another way, it is the quality of the *ethos* infusing sovereignty that is critical to political life, not the conjunction between sovereignty and biopolitics alone.

Agamben, as already implied, sometimes acts as if an account of the "logic of sovereignty" discloses ironclad paradoxes, paradoxes to be resolved only by transcending this logic. His mode of analysis engenders the eschatological gesture with which it closes. Politics and culture, however, do not possess as tight a logic as Agamben suggests. They are more littered, layered, and complex than that. The dense materiality of culture ensures that it does not correspond neatly to any design, form, pattern of efficient causality, or ironclad set of paradoxes.

Agamben displays the hubris of intellectualism when he encloses political culture within a tight logic. Some theorists express that hubris by applying a tight model of causal explanation to social processes, others by applying a closed model of historical realization, and yet others by resolving the first two images into paradoxes so tightly defined that only a radical reconstitution of the world could rise above them. All three stances understate the extent to which the complexity of biopolitical culture exceeds a consummate logic of explanation, interpretation, or paradoxicality. If you loosen Agamben's logic of paradox without eliminating it altogether you express more appreciation for the materialization of culture and locate more space to maneuver within the paradoxes he delineates. The best way to approach this issue, perhaps, is to delineate two ambiguities residing in sovereignty.

The first ambiguity, sometimes intimated by Agamben, is an equivocation inside the idea of sovereignty between acting with final authority and acting with irresistible power. This finds expression in the *OED*, in its definition of sovereignty as "supremacy in respect of power, domination, or rank; supreme dominion, authority or rule." The idea of finality runs through these terms; but in some it expresses final authority and in others irresistible effect. Both ideas find some presence in the terms "rank" and "rule." Agamben senses the difference, in his assertion that the sovereign decides the exception. But within the idea of the exception "decided" by the sovereign, an oscillation lingers between a juridical authority that decides the exception when available law is insufficient and other cultural forces that insert themselves irresistibly into the outcome.

This ambiguity inside sovereign finality finds expression in Christian theology as well as state politics. The point of the medieval nominalist critique of finalist theology is that the projection of an intrinsic purpose in the world undermines the very idea of God's omnipotence. A sovereign God, the radical devotees contended, is one touched by no intrinsic purpose limiting His power. To love God devoutly is to subtract any limit from His Being. So they attacked the doctrine through which Christian theology had bestowed political meaning, limits, and direction upon life. They expanded the sense of contingency in nature in order to obey more completely a God of absolute sovereignty. Their opponents said that this radical theology also subtracted meaning and purpose from the world over which God presided. The intensity of the debate is revealed by the fact that the future saint Thomas Aquinas was officially defined by the Church as a heretic during the heyday of nominalism.[8]

This theological debate subsists within the contemporary practice of political sovereignty. *The finality of sovereignty circulates uncertainly between authoritative sites of enunciation and irresistible forces of power.* This is not a *confusion* in the idea of sovereignty—a misunderstanding to be eliminated by a sharper definition of the term. It is, rather, the *zone of instability* that sovereignty inhabits.

The political significance of the dissonant conjunction between the effective and authoritative dimensions of sovereignty becomes apparent when linked to a second oscillation. Alexis de Tocqueville discerned it in nineteenth-century American democracy. "The principle of sovereignty of the people," he says, "which is always to be found, more or less, at the bottom of almost all human institutions, usually remains buried there."[9] In European societies, the claim of Divine Right invested sovereign authority in the king; but below that authority, enabling and confining it, were the traditions imparted to the multitude. The subterranean interplay between the multitude, tradition, and positional sovereignty enabled some initiatives by the official sovereign, resisted others, and rendered still others unthinkable.

The multitude, imperfectly infused with specific traditions, comes to the fore in a democratic regime. It helps to set the ethos in which official sovereignty is set. Better put, in democratic, constitutional states sovereignty circulates uncertainly between the multitude, traditions infused into it, and constitutionally sanctioned authorities. How would duck hunters and pickup truck drivers in the United States today, for instance, respond to a Supreme Court decision requiring that they give up all their guns? Does an unconscious anticipation of that militance influence the cases brought by plaintiffs and decisions made by the court? For that matter, what would have happened to the decision of the Gang of Five if a militant electorate, insisting that the essence of democracy requires a concerted effort to count the votes accurately in a close election, had boycotted work, blocked expressways with cars and trucks, refused jury duty, and otherwise interrupted everyday life? The dangerous confrontation would have exposed how the constitutive components of sovereignty do not always coincide. The question is not purely hypothetical, because when the recount issue was still alive the electronic news media frequently reported that there would be a vitriolic response by Republicans if the official vote count went against George W. Bush. A thick context of the thinkable and the unthinkable, the habitually expected and the impermissible, the politically acceptable and the morally outrageous, enters into authoritative readings of constitutional texts and irresistible acts of sovereign power. The micropolitics of sovereignty inhabits the subterranean circulation between these elements.

According to Tocqueville, the ethos infusing American sovereignty in the nineteenth century was above all agriculture and a Protestant, Christian tradition. That is why Amerindians could not be included in the new settler society, regardless of what the positional sovereign asserted. So when a Supreme Court decision ratified the autonomy of the Cherokee people in the Southeast, a sovereign ethos of Christian superiority personified by settler vigilante groups and the refusal by President Jackson to enforce the decision overwhelmed the positional sovereignty of the Court. The irresistible demand that European stock and Christian belief provide the basis of the Republic overturned the positional authority of the Court. Here is how Tocqueville presents the relations between the "American government" and "the white population" each time a new area was reserved by treaty for the "Indians": "Who can guarantee that they will be able to remain in peace in their new asylum? The United States pledges itself to maintain them there, but the territory they now occupy was formerly secured to them by the most solemn oaths. Now, the American government does not, it is true, take their land from them, but it allows encroachments on it. No doubt within a few years the same white population which is now pressing around them will again be on their tracks in the solitudes of Arkansas; then they will suffer again from the same ills without the same remedies; and because sooner or later there will be no land left for them, their only refuge will be the grave."[10]

Was the Court prepared to order the settlers in and around Georgia to march north and west, instead of allowing the Cherokee to be sent to Oklahoma in the march of death? Tocqueville himself had regrets about this result. But he did not dissent militantly from it because of his view that Christendom must form the first "political institution" of America. Amerindians were thus set up to be the sovereign exception, the people to be excluded from the territory they occupied first. In every territorial civilization, Tocqueville says, "there are certain great social principles which a people either introduces everywhere or tolerates nowhere."[11] Strict constructionists implicitly seek a return of that culture of sovereignty. To them a strict reading of the constitution inserts a conservative rendering of Christianity into the ethos of sovereignty.

The sovereign process that Tocqueville describes already invested the eighteenth and nineteenth centuries in a fateful conjunction between biopolitics and sovereignty. The living space available to Amerindians was squeezed by the effective sovereignty over the land by Christian settlers. But the circulation that Tocqueville charts does not fit the tight logic that Agamben characterizes. *If* a political movement, drawing part of its sustenance from another dimension of Christian faith, had successfully altered the ethos in which Presidents governed, courts decided, and settlers responded to court decisions, the paradox of sovereignty would remain, biopolitics would persist, and the relevant constitutional language would still be insufficient to judicial decisions. But the alternative ethos would incline the confluence of court decisions and popular action in a different direction. Citizen participation in the ethos of sovereignty takes place through the micropolitics of sovereignty.

So the practice of sovereignty is composed by a plurality of elements—an oscillation between irresistible power and official authority and between the official site of sovereignty and the institutionally embedded ethos flowing into it. But would it not be more rigorous to cleanse the concept of this litter? Isn't sovereignty inflated into all of politics if you do not? My judgment is that it is possible to minimize the risk by focusing sovereignty on pivotal moments when final decisions are needed. It is precisely during such moments that the elements we have dissected reverberate back and forth. When the next sharp turn in time arrives, when a sovereign decision is needed and established precedents are insufficient—these elements will again enter into circulation. They will form a protracted crystal of time from which the next settlement of sovereignty emerges. It is better, then, to include inside the concept the elements that enter into this circulation. Even though the conceptual cleansing operation will eventually fail, the attempt to accomplish it dampens citizens' efforts to participate in the shape of sovereignty.

The relevance of this point to the contemporary world is underlined by reviewing its connection to the Nazi Holocaust, the key example informing Agamben's study. The conjunction of biopolitics and Article 48 of the Weimar Republic did not alone generate the Nazi Holocaust against Jews, the Romana, and homosexuals. A series of intense relays between those factors and a political culture suffused with antisemitism and resentment against defeat in the First World War generated the devastating result. Without this vengeful ethos of sovereignty, the conjunction between biopolitics and Article 48 might have turned out differently. An ethos of sovereignty is both external to sovereignty and internal to sovereignty, both part of it and one of its cultural conditions of being.

Gilles Deleuze and Felix Guattari concur in the perspective advanced here. Agreeing that there is a rift at the center of sovereignty, they nonetheless find fascism to flow from a series of "resonances" between state action, fascist gangs, and a large segment of the populace providing passive support to fascism. They speak to the micropolitics by which that ethos of sovereignty was consolidated, allowing the negative case of fascism to provide clues to the corollary importance of micropolitics to a pluralist ethos of sovereignty: "But fascism is inseparable from the proliferation of molecular focuses in interaction, which skip from point to point to point, *before* beginning to resonate together in the National Socialist State. Rural fascism and city or neighborhood fascism, youth fascism and war veteran's fascism, fascism of the Left and fascism of the Right, fascism of the couple, family, school, and office: every fascism is defined by a micro–black hole that stands on its own and communicates with the others, before resonating in a great, generalized, central black hole . . . Even after the National Socialist State had been established, microfascisms persisted that gave it unequaled ability to act upon the 'masses.' "[12]

Pluralist Democracy and Sovereignty

The sovereign is not simply (as Agamben and Schmitt tend to say) *he* (or *she*) who first decides that there is an exception and then decides how to resolve it.[13] Sovereign is *that* which decides an exception exists and how to decide it, with the *that* composed of a plurality of forces circulating through and under the positional sovereignty of the official arbitrating body. Such a result may discourage those who seek a tight explanation of the economic and political causes of legal action (the realists), a closed model of legal process (the idealists), or a tight model of legal paradox (the paradoxicalists). But it illuminates the complexity of sovereignty. It has another advantage, too: it points to strategic issues and sites to address for those who seek to introduce a robust pluralism into the ethos of sovereignty.

In American democracy sovereignty circulates uncertainly between a Supreme Court now sanctioned *positionally* (after an early period of struggle and radical self-assertion) to decide contested issues authoritatively, a populace marked by an uneven distribution of power, and orientations to religious life and other traditions into which the populace is inducted. Today one such tradition is protection of the integrity of national elections, as an expression of the most elemental act of democratic citizenship. If that tradition is abrogated, much else about democracy is placed in jeopardy. So when the Gang of Five stopped the vote count before it was necessary to do so, it exercised positional sovereignty to curtail the democratic element in the civilizational ethos of sovereignty. The Gang gave priority to a candidate over partisanship for democracy in a setting where other possible decisions were consistent with the porous words of the law and Constitution.

What of those, like me, who protest this action? Do we not owe the Court respect and obedience nonetheless, precisely because it occupies a position critical to constitutional democracy? We owe *positional* respect to the institution called upon to make authoritative decisions when the pressure of time compels them. That responsibility is met by a presumption of obedience to Court decisions and by public admission that democratic constitutionalism needs such a body in a non-parliamentary system. But to express partiality for democracy is to accept other responsibilities as well: to reveal how the negotiation of sovereign decisions draws upon a larger ethos; to expose the duplicity of those who preach strict constructionism in general and then point to the situation at hand as if it were unique in being underprecedented; to publicize how the constitutive ambiguity between positional and cultural sovereignty was exploited in this case by the Gang of Five; and to struggle for a more democratic and pluralistic ethos of sovereignty. When the investment of sovereignty in a larger ethos is appreciated, it becomes clear how important it is to struggle for a generous ethos in which positional sovereignty operates. We meet our first responsibility to sovereignty by a presumption to obedience that might be overridden on some occasions; we meet the second by contesting publicly the partisanship against democracy exercised by the Gang of Five.

There is a related issue. An ethos of sovereignty appropriate to the contemporary condition is not merely one that displays partiality for the integrity of democratic elections. It must also *become* one that points beyond the implicit connection between the drive to Christian superiority and strict construction of constitutional provisions. For an exclusionary definition of Christian orthodoxy sets the ethos in which strict constructionism is practiced, an ethos which numerous bicameral Christian citizens contest in the name of pluralism. In this respect a Supreme Court justice such as Antonin Scalia agrees with Tocqueville of the early nineteenth century, though it is rather doubtful that a contemporary Tocqueville would continue to concur with Scalia. Tocqueville found Protestant

Christianity to play a compelling role in the ethos of sovereignty in nineteenth-century America. He might well respond differently today, as the diversity of theistic and nontheistic faiths on the same territory continues to grow.

A lot has happened between 1830 and today. Stirred by the compression of distance through the acceleration of pace, biopolitical culture has bumped through several transformations. A new plurality of religious and nonreligious orientations forms a constitutive part of biopolitical culture today. To renegotiate the ethos of sovereignty in the contemporary context requires an audacious pluralization of the sacred and a corollary relaxation of what it takes to defile the sense of the sacred embraced by you, me, or others. Such a political project is demanding. But no more so than earlier drives to incorporate a new plurality within Protestant Christianity, or, after that, to fashion a more secular public culture, or, after that, to appreciate the wider heritage of Judeo-Christian culture, or, after that, to accept a broader range of ethnic diversity. When partisans of this or that confessional faith draw a specific confession of the sacred into public life, as most regularly do today, it becomes legitimate for others to contest some of its assumptions publicly and to explore critically pertinent aspects of its texts and rituals if the confessors seek to apply those dictates to everyone.

The demanding tasks are, first, to maintain presumptive respect for positional sovereignty, second, to pluralize the number of legitimate existential faiths (including non-Christian and nontheistic faiths) within the ethos of sovereignty, and third, to relax what *counts* as an assault upon the sacred confessed by you or others.

The project is to generalize partiality for democracy and to fold agonistic respect between diverse constituencies into the ethos of sovereignty. A launching pad for that project is the understanding that positional sovereignty is both indispensable to the rule of law and constitutively insufficient to itself. It is both conditioned by, and expressive of, an entrenched ethos. The contemporary need is to instill an ethos of bicameralism into military, church, police, educational, judicial, corporate, labor, and executive institutions.[14] The struggle to negotiate a generous ethos of pluralism expresses the respect that democrats bestow upon the indispensability and uncertainty of sovereignty.

The Global Dimension of Sovereignty

We have yet, however, to come to terms with another complexity in sovereignty that grows more acute by the day. That is the way in which it increasingly stretches beyond the internal structure of the state to encompass extrastate processes as well.

Sovereignty has long revealed a double face as well as an ambiguous profile. For internal state sovereignty rests to a significant degree upon whether other states recognize a regime to be sovereign. Moreover, classic theorists of sovereignty such as Hegel contend that the sovereignty of most states is always partial and limited. For a system of sovereign states to flourish a "world historical state" must emerge to limit, enable, and regulate the quasi-sovereignty of the other states. Even to accept Hegel's thesis, however, would still be to obscure the extent to which sovereignty today exceeds the reach of any historical state, even a world historical state. For sovereignty now implicates suprastate institutions and capitalist processes that confine and channel state and interstate activities.

Some theorists would say that this layer of suprastate power, to the extent that it has arrived, announces the death of sovereignty. But Michael Hardt and Antonio Negri call such announcements into question. They suggest, wisely, that sovereignty itself becomes more complex today. More than Rousseau, Tocqueville, and Agamben, Hardt and Negri reflect upon the global dimension of sovereignty.[15] Their analysis, even if one questions its details, discloses both an additional level of sovereignty and new sites of citizen action appropriate to it.

Hardt and Negri claim that a new world order has emerged out of recent developments in capitalism and the remains of European imperialism. Their project, in the first instance, is to map and explain these institutional developments. In the second instance, it is to pursue the "transformation" of this world assemblage.

The most salutary contribution that Hardt and Negri make is in the map that charts the migration of sovereignty to a layered global assemblage in which leading capitalist states, transnational corporations, supranational regulatory institutions, and global media networks are components. Here is one summary of the layered assemblage that they name

Empire: "First and foremost, then, the concept of Empire posits a regime that effectively encompasses the spatial totality of the civilized world . . . Second . . . Empire presents itself not as a historical regime originating in conquest but rather as an order that effectively suspends history and thereby fixes the existing state of affairs for eternity . . . Third, the rules of Empire operate on all registers of the social order extending down to the depths of the social world . . . Finally, although the practice of Empire is continually bathed in blood—the concept of Empire is always dedicated to peace—a perpetual and universal peace outside of history."[16]

The charting of this assemblage in *Empire* makes fascinating reading. Its multiple organs and levels render the assemblage both powerful and unsteady. It is easy to identify a hegemonic state within Empire—the United States—but less easy to identify a world historical state presiding over a world of semisovereign states. For the hegemon itself is contained and channeled by a variety of cross-state institutions and processes. The United States, moved by one desire to determine its destiny unfettered by other states and a conflicting desire to lead the rest in shaping extra-state institutions, is often pulled kicking and screaming into serving the new world order. Empire regulates and constrains it, even as it sits on the "narrow pinnacle" at its apex.[17] Hardt's and Negri's analysis of the United States in relation to suprastate institutions mirrors the relation between formal and civilizational sovereignty that Tocqueville mapped inside nineteenth-century America.[18]

There is a broad, second layer just below the pinnacle. The corporate system of capital, linked through mergers, market interdependencies, overlapping boards of directors, the priority of the commodity relation, managerial mobility, common techniques of management, investment priorities, common financial instruments, and media control, sets a thick layer of global governance, entering into state priorities, investment decisions, work routines, habits of judgment, and moral propensities. These "huge transnational corporations construct the connective fabric of the biopolitical world . . . they directly structure and articulate territories and populations."[19] This layer constrains states as well as serving them. There are also the numerous supranational financial, governing, and judicial agencies that serve and regulate the global economy.

I will not review the map further, even though the details are fascinating. For there are critical omissions on it. First, institutional religion plays no significant role. It is sometimes ignored and at others treated as a mere proxy for supervening forces such as the expansion of capital into new zones of life or the mobilization of resistance to the expansion of capital. This comes out as Hardt and Negri insist, against impressive evidence to the contrary, that the belief in transcendence has lost its ability to inspire fear and hope in the late modern world. "Today there is not even the illusion of a transcendent God . . . The poor has dissolved the image and recuperated its power."[20] Or when they say that "every metaphysical tradition is now completely worn out." You might forget for a moment that Hardt lives in the United States, the western state where many constituencies organize much of their political lives around Christian faith. It emerges also in their refusal to ask what role religious faith plays in the contested politics of the multitude. The multitude, for them, is a reservoir of passion and potential political energy under-colonized by Empire. Surely Christianity, Islam, Judaism, Hinduism, and Buddhism play a role on the world stage that exceeds defining them as dependent phenomena. They enter into the passions of the multitude, if anything does. And they help to shape institutional governance at every level. Think, for instance, about Talal Asad's account, reviewed in chapter 2, of how European secularism is grounded in a historical modification of Christianity that does not mesh well with the evolution of Islamic or Hindu practices. And these institutions sometimes generate impressive resistance to the priorities of Empire. Why is religion relegated to a minor role in the map of *Empire*?

Second, NGOs such as Greenpeace, Amnesty International, Oxfam, and Shanti Sena, treated by others as modes of pressure to restrain or move dominant forces in the world order, are construed by Hardt and Negri as subordinate partners of Empire. "Here, at this broadest, most universal level, the activities of these NGOs coincide with the workings of Empire, 'beyond politics,' on the terrain of biopower, meeting the needs of life itself."[21] The idea seems to be that in responding to crises of hunger, or publicizing abuse and torture of prisoners of war, or providing health services, these organizations protect Empire from radical opposition. Perhaps they do. But surely they are more ambiguous in actuality and possibility than that. What presses the authors to categorize them so categorically?

The depreciation of transnational religious energy and the confinement of NGOs to supporting roles within Empire expose a deep ambivalence running throughout Hardt's and Negri's account. Two conflicting drives govern it. There is one drive to play up (in a Deleuzian manner) the uncertainties, porosities, and open future of Empire when it is *mapped* as an assemblage. There is another, counter drive to treat it (in a classic, Marxist way) as a more closed structure of domination when it is *appraised* as a site of potential transformation. I find the map to be illuminating. But as I read the strategic narrative I am reminded of that delicious scene in *The Life of Brian*, when the revolutionary leader against Rome asks a leading question to his comrades huddled together in the catacombs, "What have the Romans ever done for us?" "Well, they built the aqueducts," blurts out one member huddling with him. "Yes, but besides the aqueducts, What have the Romans ever done for us?" "An education system," another mole shouts. We return much later to a laundry list of Roman accomplishments, reviewed in precise order by the meticulous leader, followed by the refrain, "Besides the aqueducts, education system, peace," etc., etc. . . . "What have the Romans *ever* done for us?" My question to Hardt and Negri is, "What has Empire, as you map it before translating the map into a strategic blueprint, done for many of the values that you seek to advance?" I pose the question not to forgo vigorous critique of several dimensions of the emerging world order, but to call into question the wisdom of huddling in a corner waiting for "the multitude" to bring the edifice down.

The gap between the map and the strategic blueprint discloses how Deleuze and Marx are not, as the authors promise, folded into each other. Rather, each is given priority in turn, as the text shuffles back and forth between charting the loose structure of Empire and identifying the multitude as its protean, implacable opponent.[22] Now we can discern why religion is downgraded and NGOs are degraded. The narrative depreciation of religion is needed to clear conceptual space to identify a virtual multitude as the implacable enemy of Empire. For if religion were endowed with more agency and ambiguity in the interior of the multitude itself, its potential susceptibility to multiple possibilities of action would spring more sharply into view. It would become a vital object of contestation, not simply a potential force of transformation. And the location of NGOs entirely *within* Empire? That is a sign of the authors' unwillingness to translate porosities and uncertain potentialities discernible on their *map* into positive possibilities of *strategic citizen action* to twist capital, cross-state regulatory agencies, and religious organizations in more positive directions.[23]

In contrast to Hardt and Negri, I adopt much of the map that they present without embracing the strategic rhetoric they advance. To me, Empire is an ambiguous, porous assemblage containing positive supports and possibilities as well as ugly modes of domination and danger. It is potentially susceptible to reconfiguration through the cumulative effect of selective state actions, changes of policy by international institutions, and militant cross-state citizen action. There would be disaster were it to collapse, as it could perhaps do through a combination of internal crises, preemptive wars by the United States, and terrorist actions that disrupt the web holding it together. That being said, it is also imperative to contest many of its priorities at each level of organization. Sometimes NGOs and religious organizations can play pivotal roles in that contestation. At other times they are part of the problem. Deleuze got it right. Empire is a loose world assemblage to be tracked and challenged at numerous points in efforts to twist its uncertain and porous structure in more positive directions.

The strategic side of Hardt's and Negri's ambivalence finds most dramatic expression in their identification of "the multitude" as a fugitive, mobile force that could transform Empire. The multitude assumes on a world scale the function that the revolutionary version of Marxism once invested in the proletariat, though it does not have the same composition. Its task is transformation. But because Empire is also so pervasive and so retrograde nothing specific can be said by the authors about the direction that the transformation should take. It is not just that they have not got around to this assignment. Rather, their strategic orientation itself makes it both imperative and impossible. Here are a few samples of what the authors say:

Furthermore, we have not yet been able to give any coherent indication of what type of political subjectivities might contest and overthrow the forces of Empire.

Even when we manage to touch on the productive, ontological dimension . . . and the resistances that arise there, we will still not be in a position—not even at the end of this book—to point to any already existing and concrete elaboration of a political alternative to Empire . . . It will only arise in practice.

"What we need is to create a new social body, which is a project that goes well beyond refusal. Our lines of flight . . . create a real alternative . . ., humanity squared, enriched by a collective intelligence and love of the community" [their italics].

This is the point when the modern republic ceases to exist and the postmodern posse arises. This is the founding moment of an earthly city that is strong and distinct from any divine city . . . Only the multitude through its practical experimentation will offer the models and determine when and how the possible becomes real.[24]

In presenting their strategic imaginary Hardt and Negri say that "contingency, mobility and flexibility" are Empire's real strength, thereby disparaging at the outset ambiguous forces in it that might reshape it in some way. It appears that "collective intelligence and love of the community" can, for them, only subsist below institutional life. No wonder they cannot give "any indication" of the shape of the "new subjectivities" they demand. It is necessary to move beyond, first, identifying critical energies entirely with a fugitive constituency called "the multitude"; second, assuming that critical action is inevitably sucked into the tedious game of bare repetition unless it is transformative; and third, refusing to specify in advance the proximate goals of cross-state citizen movements.[25]

The dilemma they have created comes out poignantly in Michael Hardt's participation during the spring of 2002 in a symposium sponsored by *Theory & Event* on 9/11. Hardt issues a brief statement on how the "tragic event" signifies the possible emergence of a "civil war" in Empire: "In order for the 11 September attack or the responses to it to be acts of war, there would have to be two sovereign powers confronting one another. Since there are not, then these can only be considered acts of a civil war, that is, conflict within the space of one single sovereignty."[26]

Insightfully, the fight between terrorists and dominant states is defined as a civil war. But where is the fire displayed in the book? Does the cooling occur because Hardt can neither embrace the event, nor oppose it vociferously, nor call for specific responses to it? He may hesitate to *oppose* the attack vociferously because Al Qaeda embodies the network mode of organization and intense oppositional energy that marks the multitude. A civil war, focused on the "nerve centers" of Empire, might be just the thing to dismantle it. But Hardt, to his credit, recoils from this conclusion. He fails to *embrace* the event because, no doubt, he cringes from its violence and because Al Qaeda, even as it embodies traits of the multitude, participates in a "fundamentalist" formation that he finds unacceptable. Finally, he cannot commend reform of the global assemblage in the aftermath of 9/11 because given the *strategic* face of his reading, Empire is too fixed and bankrupt to be amenable to reform. Hence a brief, cool statement, in which the contrasting terms "tragic event" and "civil war" stare bleakly out at the reader.

The Global Dimension of Citizenship

A positive rejoinder to Hardt and Negri could be pursued with respect to critical cross-state issues of child labor, global warming, indigenous peoples, prostitution rings, labor movements, emission standards, preemptive state wars, the Geneva Conventions on prisoners of war, religious freedom, income disparities between North and South, and legal and illegal population flows across borders. The point to emphasize is that today creative citizen action must track the contemporary complexity of sovereignty. Citizens must address plural sites of action, depending

on the scope of the issue, including local action, associational organization, state pressure, and cross-state citizen networks. Let's focus on the
last site through the issue of terrorism as crystallized through the events
of 9/11.

As a Deleuzian with a liberal streak, I have an ambivalence in my
thinking that differs from that of Hardt and Negri. To me, 9/11 and the
American response reveal how fragile the supranational system of governance is in its justice and injustices; therefore, how important it is to
draw upon some of these institutions when the "pinnacle" state becomes
reckless; furthermore, how disastrous it would be if that porous assemblage were to collapse through internal crisis, the military adventur-
ism of one country, or terrorist activity aimed at critical points of conjunction; moreover, how open Empire might be to twists and turns that
speak more eloquently to the needs of the time than it now does; and
thereby, how incumbent it is upon critical intellectuals, religious leaders,
liberal film actors, technical workers, and assorted professionals in predominantly Christian, Jewish, and Islamic states to mobilize cross-state
citizen coalitions to oppose the state terrorism of the Likud Party in
Israel, to resist preemptive wars by the United States, and to press for a
contiguous state of Palestine.[27] The idea is to support selective police
action against Al Qaeda while addressing the unbearable humiliations
that pull Islamic recruits into the movement and foster more widespread
passive support for it.

The critical intellectuals and professionals invoked here do not compose the multitude; they are sunk up to their necks in Empire. For that
very reason, they can coalesce to press the assemblage in new directions.
Today it is imperative to insist that the policies of Israel, the United
States, and Hamas are coalescing to foster Palestinian humiliation and
hopelessness from which the networks of Al Qaeda and like-minded
organizations are forged, financed, and supported. It is because we participate in the state and interstate machinery through which this politics
of humiliation is forged that it is possible and obligatory to mobilize our
states, corporations, universities, theaters, public media, and temples to
exert new pressure for change.

As a pluralist, my highest ideal would be a greater state made up of
citizens now in the state of Israel and the occupied territories. A state in

which all members have full rights of citizenship. One argument in support of that agenda is the extensive intermixing of populations and institutions on both sides of the border. But to make that project work there would have to be significant factions in both Israel and the occupied territory who support it. Citizen activists outside each territory could then join them to press the United States, Israel, Palestine, and the UN to move in that direction.

But my sense is that there is not now a critical mass on the ground ready to support a pluralistic, one-state agenda.[28] So to relieve the suffering and humiliation now, it seems best to press for a state of Palestine, doing so in a way that maximizes future chances for pluralism within both states. We must join critical activists inside Palestine and Israel to press for a state of Palestine; for providing it with the same amount of material and financial support currently bestowed upon Israel; for the security of both states guaranteed by an international military force; and for equal citizenship for all minorities in each state.

My major concern, however, is less with the exact shape that such a settlement might take and more with the pressures needed to compel the parties to reach a settlement. The United States is unlikely to take a militant lead in this project without external pressure, for the formula of electoral success of each political party pulls it away from doing so. The United States requires as much internal and external pressure as the Israeli regime.

What shape can such a cross-state citizen movement take? It will be composed, above all, of free-thinking intellectuals, religious leaders, actors, and professionals in and around the states and institutional faiths actively involved in the conflict. It will mobilize pressure upon the states and corporate structures in which its members participate to compel Israel to accept a state of Palestine and to inform the "settlers" whom Israel has placed there over several decades that they can either return to Israel or live in the new state of Palestine. It will publicize courageous actions within Israel and Palestine that the news media in the United States obscure, such as that taken by the Israeli pilots in 2003 who refused to participate in future bombing missions over Palestine. And it will publicize the work of post-Zionists within Israel who have reexamined the official history of how the population already there was dispersed when Israel was formed. It is true that the Holocaust in Europe placed the world under a profound obligation to found a state of Israel. But grave injustices were also done to the people already on the ground; and their departure from Israel was forced through tough policies. Uri Ram, a professor at Ben Gurion University, summarizes the new exploration of the historical record: "In the conventional view, Israel is considered to have always been peace-seeking and given to compromise while the Arab states are portrayed as stubborn aggressors. The new historians argue that the state of Israel declined opportunities for negotiation with Arab states, but on the other hand concluded an unwritten pact with the Jordanian kingdom to parcel between the two the territory known as the West Bank, so as to prevent the establishment of a Palestinian state there . . . Furthermore, new historians argue that Israel bears a large . . . responsibility for the creation of the Palestinian refugee problem. It is argued that during Israel's war of independence in 1948 Israeli military commanders . . . evicted hundreds of thousands of Palestinians from their villages and expelled them beyond the state's borders."[29]

These are actions that need to be rectified, even as we evince appreciation of the horrendous Holocaust that pressed some of them into being. To do so it is critical to rewrite popular memory of this history in Israel and the United States. For creative action in the present is always bound to the memories from which it proceeds.

It will take pressure within the churches, temples, universities, and corporations to which participants belong to compel state and international agencies to withhold material support from Israel until it accepts a state of Palestine. Such a movement will assert forcefully that the pursuit of that state must not be stymied either by new terrorist action by Hamas *or* new acts of state terrorism by the Likud government, as these two opposing forces collude to break attempts to form a state of Palestine. And it will press the United States, from inside and outside its borders, to decrease dependence upon Arab oil, to support the Kyoto Protocol, to promote policies of energy efficiency at home, to publicize the Geneva Accord between residents of Israel and Palestine, and to make future financial aid to Israel dependent upon its recognition of a state of Palestine. Such a cross-state collection of independent leaders and professionals strives to tap the energies of larger constituencies so that they too will apply critical pressure upon their states, temples, and selves. It will push states such as France, England, Japan, and Egypt, from inside and outside, to put more pressure upon the United States, Israel, and Palestine to reach a settlement.

Perhaps a cross-state citizen campaign of divestment from Israeli corporations is needed until the regime changes its policies. Perhaps divestment from American oil companies and automobile corporations that refuse to build hybrid cars is needed. Mock international tribunals can be established to try state and nonstate terrorists. And actors, models, and publicists of international stature can sponsor shows, commercials, film documentaries, fashion shows, and so on that mix into their music, acting, and erotica political facts and proposals that counter those offered by right-wing moguls in the United States who dominate the electronic news media. It is upon our ability to tap the *intensive* energies of *pluralizing* forces in Judaism, Islam, Christianity, Israel, Palestine, the United States, and Europe that the best hope to reshape this dimension of Empire resides. The networks of communication that Empire engenders, and that Hardt and Negri identify so effectively, can be deployed on behalf of this effort.

Such an effort may fail, but it will not be because the structures of Empire make success impossible. It will be because the energies and tactics generated are insufficient at this time to move the inertia of Empire in this way rather than another.

In other cases too, where Hardt and Negri embrace implacable resistance on behalf of vague transformation, a better course is an energetic politics of citizen pressure within and above traditional state politics, pressure designed to move states and corporations in directions resisted by the inertia of Empire. The guiding idea is that the structures and priorities of Empire are not set in stone, even though the power distribution is heavily weighted. For the order of global capital conforms neatly neither to the logic of self-regulation and light state monetary policy commended by classical economists nor to that of necessary crisis elaborated by its revolutionary opponents. Therefore, it might be turned in new directions by an effective combination of institutional regulation, vital citizen movements, and revised state priorities. The point is to exude neither pessimism nor optimism about the future. Those are spectatorial stances. It is, rather, to challenge existing priorities even if the *probabilities* of full success are low, because the world's *need* to progress on these fronts is so urgent and the current state and suprastate incentives are weak.

One reason why modern capitalism has resisted both precise management and revolutionary overthrow is that its organization and trajectory exceed the smooth theories advanced by moderate economists and the system of contradictions identified by theorists of crisis. Proponents of each theory purport to know more about these jury-rigged processes than their uncertain trajectory allows. *Moreover, that which is not formed by a tight logic or design is also unlikely to succumb to a simple logic of management, revolution, or transformation.* Hardt and Negri almost see this, but not as deeply or consistently as do two of their purported guides, Deleuze and Foucault.

Transformation is neither needed nor in the cards today; what is needed is creative modes of *intervention* posed at several strategic sites in the service of reducing economic inequality, fostering intra- and interstate pluralism, and promoting ecological sanity. Such energies, aimed at slippery and mobile targets, will meet with failure and surprise on many occasions. That is because they enter into currents of power that while weighted against them, exceed any agency's full control. It is mere hubris of state leaders, transnational bureaucrats, neoclassical economics professors, neorealist IR theorists, or Marxist intellectuals to say otherwise. Again, James, Bergson, Deleuze, and Foucault know better. They realize that the world exceeds any system of explanation or control brought to bear on it. They strive to *intervene* creatively and proximately in events, not to know or master them from beginning to end or start to finish.

Thus the most compelling contributions that Hardt and Negri make are in mapping another layer onto the politics of sovereignty and in opening a dialogue between heretofore separate traditions of inquiry into global politics. Their most serious deficiencies consist in a failure to pursue that dialogue far and a refusal to compose a strategic response beyond the empty politics of transformation by the multitude. Michel Foucault was also attuned to modes of critical action that exceed extant institutional channels. Here is a formulation by him that, once elevated to the global register, helps to define the cross-state citizen activism needed today. It speaks to those who appreciate the ambiguities circulating through state sovereignty, discern the global dimension of sovereignty, and seek levers of citizen action at each node through which the complexity of sovereignty circulates: "There's an optimism that consists in saying that things couldn't be better. My optimism would consist rather in saying that so many things can be changed, fragile as they are, bound up more with circumstances than necessities, more arbitrary than self-evident, more a matter of complex, but temporary, historical circumstances than of inevitable anthropological constants . . . You know, to say that we are much more recent than we think, is to place at the disposal of the work that we can do on ourselves the greatest share of what is presented to us as inaccessible."[30]

Postlude

BELONGING
TO TIME

Today the durability of democracy is tied to the pluralization of life within Euro-American states and the reconstitution of relations between Judeo-Christian and Islamic traditions. One way to probe the pertinent connections is to address those perspectives that press against deep pluralism. Another is to articulate the positive possibility itself. We have pursued each strategy in this study. It may be timely now to shift gears again. For we are teachers, writers, students, and thinkers. Many of us are already inclined toward pluralism. Can more be done to deepen our own feeling for it?

William James, Henri Bergson, Gilles Deleuze, Talal Asad, the Dalai Lama, and Marcel Proust, disagreeing among themselves on several matters, concur on the importance of practice, sensibility, and ethos to thinking, judgment, and courage. Each, in his way, criticizes the sufficiency of intellectualism to philosophy, political theory, faith, and thinking; each ponders how to enliven the dispositions through which perception is colored, concepts are formed, evidence is sifted, interpretation is engaged, arguments are inflected, and faith is consolidated. In these figures you can also hear echoes from the likes of Buddha, Lucretius, Jesus, Spinoza, and Nietzsche. They too advance different creeds while jointly emphasizing the relevance of practice to the sensibility infusing a creed.

The fact that we inhabit a time when the acceleration of pace and the fragility of being are both palpable may itself point to a timely way to pursue these connections further. Maybe amplification of the sense of belonging to time provides a way to deepen the feeling for pluralism.

In November 2002 I saw *The Maltese Falcon* at the Charles Theater in Baltimore, in the company of an anonymous gang of Baltimore film buffs. It is the role of repetition in that collective experience which fascinates me. The audience, ranging in age from thirty to seventy, received the film six decades after its first showing in 1941. Many had viewed it on DVD or television after its date of issue. But we were now assembled together, as an anonymous crowd, most seeing the film for a second or third time.

We sink into the story with pleasure, reserving a bit of time to fold appreciation of some differences between then and now into that pleasure. We chuckle as the hot, upper-class babe tells her story of distress to Sam. The chuckle grows loud as we realize we are sharing the thought that the scene did not draw a smile from the audience the first time around. That audience had not encountered this "type" several times, nor had they read articles about how it limits women. Her duplicity was not so transparent then, or so we surmise through our laughter. We soon take audible pleasure in the impending romance between Sam and her, before we are supposed to do so.

Later, we laugh when Spade knocks Peter Lorre out cold with one short, quick jab to the head. No brutal beating here; no gunfight consuming ten minutes of screen time. When Lorre recovers a few minutes later none the worse for wear, we express benign amusement again. Sam, with only a trace of the Bogart grimace that becomes pronounced in later films, is now free to make a quick deal with him, taking advantage of Lorre's desperate quest for the Falcon.

We repeatedly squirm in anticipation as the film signals some turn of fate, convinced that the initial audience received those signals more as infra-percepts to ponder later through flashbacks than overt signs of what was coming. Perhaps we are too smug for our own good. No matter: the recognition that we may be encourages even more smiles. Later we laugh again when the good cop shows too much adulation for Spade by today's standards because of Sam's prowess in solving cases; and then again when the bad cop exudes anxiety anytime the private sleuth is around.

All these chuckles, laughs, and smiles while immersed in the turns and twists of the plot, some of which surprise us again. We laugh out loud during a late scene, when the head cop carefully drapes that expensive fur coat over the guilty woman's shoulders, displaying how high she had been and how far she is falling before our very eyes. We laugh once more with self-satisfied glee when the elevator bars slide down in front of the woman, as she is escorted to a life in prison with thicker bars.

Sam is now free of the law and love entanglements. He is free to roam the next time a sexy, duplicitous woman walks into his office desperately seeking help. Oooh, Sam . . .

The contemporary experience of the film is doubled. There is a mirroring back and forth between one time and another. We inhabit the space between those mirrors, as it were, reflecting each into the other. Our experience is doubled, and then doubled again, as we now look into a mirror of the past and then glimpse the present from the vantage point of the past. Now and then; then and now. But that characterization is not quite sufficient: our experience consists of a series of rapid resonances or reverberations rolling back and forth between first and second viewings, infused with historical events now burned into the visceral register of collective experience.

What can we make of these reverberations once pulled to the foreground of attention? Some reviewers will dissolve them in the soup of nostalgia. The contemporary viewers, they say, wish they were living then. But such a judgment merely adds another ripple to the open spiral of reverberations. Others will say that the contemporary viewer is governed by a questionable sense of superiority: We are not as knowing, ironic, and self-reflective as we think. Others will see the film through the lens of ideology-critique, saying that it reveals a cultural unconscious in need of overcoming, or recouping, or selective restaging.

Let's pass by the nostalgists, ironists, ideology-critics, and cynics this time around, even though insights can be found in their approaches. Too much concentration on those conceits obscures something else critical to lived experience. One way to put the point is that experience, to be experience, must shuffle back and forth between the past from the vantage point of the present and the present from the vantage point of the past, as they mingle, collide, collude, and lurch toward an uncertain future. The shuffle involves an uncertain series of movements to and fro, inside the same perception, the same thought, the same judgment, the same hope, the same fear, the same pleasure, the same laugh, and the same sense of ambivalence. Those bursts of laughter at the Charles, for instance, well up before the audience can say what makes this or that scene funny. A series of rapid, layered reverberations between the first and second events crystallizes experience.

The viewing encourages us to ponder the temporal character of experience rather than push that dimension into the shadows to harvest the results of experience. The first time we saw the film, the uneasy coexistence of past and present was placed under the shadow of an uncertain future to which the reverberations pointed. The later viewing thus spawns a more vivid experience, an experience in which the pressure of the future is relaxed, an experience in which we can dwell more actively in the reverberations themselves.

The viewing of *The Maltese Falcon* in 2002 secretes collective crystals of time, organized across several decades of chrono-time. It brings out the vivacity of temporality to life, even as we keep one eye and ear honed on the plot line. What is the effect of such indwelling?

Waking Life, a more recent film, does not require repetition between past and current viewings to do its work. Its cartoon characters consist of wavy, undulating figures, drawn in ink, who flow across the screen like ghosts floating through the mist of Dartmoor in southwest England. The liquid characters slipping in and out of the screen ponder the meaning of life, or in some cases the investments put into it. At one point someone announces that the brain lives for six minutes after the body dies. Suddenly the thought arises that the film itself *is* this six minutes in the life of a person. It *is* a protracted experience of pure duration, where thoughts, memories, feelings, and judgments from different people and periods mingle, each located on several registers of being at the same time. This mingling is unmoored from the chronological order in which the events appeared; it is also untethered to the future action of the character. Mobility, action, and an extended future are not in the cards during this live postmortem.

Thinking mixes affect, feeling, memories, and ideas into a qualitative ensemble indissoluble into separate "parts." This time, the mixing itself assumes center stage. The uncanny effect of the film is to enliven the experience of life as you are plunged into the experience of duration through which memories, thoughts, and judgments regularly melt into one another below the attention of future-oriented actors. You may begin to dwell joyously upon that implicit attachment to the complexity of time that underpins life. The opinions that different characters espouse, while they sometimes solicit your judgment, now take second place to the process by which they are sifted and folded into the compass of being. You dwell in the experience of becoming that unfolds more vividly in a world now severed from operational imperatives of perception, judgment, action, and responsibility. You dwell in an experience that normally inhabits the background of life. As you do so, you may sense how a slight twist here or there could have turned your experience in a different direction. You become more sensitized to a few forks not pursued as well as to some that were. You begin to feel the link between plurality and belonging to time.

Duration can be interpreted in multiple ways, with some interpretations carrying you to the idea of a whole that is open and others to the idea of timelessness against which the flux of duration is set. These differences—let us label them the magnificence of transcendence within immanence or the wonder of immanence without transcendence—may emerge as alternative inflections of a more generic experience of belonging to time, with each honed by the official doctrine and ritual practices appropriate to it. The fact that belonging to time can be inflected in different ways may now begin to find expression in the experience itself.

We addressed in chapter 4 the relations that Bergson poses between duration, becoming, causality, meaning, politics, and ethics. But as you slide into the experiences these two films solicit, and then dwell again upon the subtle lessons issuing from indwelling, a related response becomes more palpable. Here is how Bergson puts it: "What was immobile and frozen in our perception is warmed and set in motion. Everything comes to life around us and is revivified in us . . . We feel ourselves uplifted, carried away, borne along by it. We are made more fully alive and this increase of life brings with it the conviction that grave philosophical enigmas can be resolved."[1]

Let's bypass Bergson's claim that the practice of indwelling (he calls it "intuition") can resolve deep philosophical contests. He seems to me to overstate that case, since the experience could be interpreted through the lens of finalism or that of becoming, with several stopping points in between. Besides, he qualifies that confidence in another work, as we saw in chapter 4. But note his assertion that life becomes "warmed," "set in motion," "revivified," and "uplifted" as you dwell in duration. That is an effect induced by *Waking Life* the first time you see it and *The Maltese Falcon* the second and third times. Dwelling in duration affects the sensibilities through which we act. And it can prime us to do more work yet upon them. It does so by drawing attention to the complexity of the process by which attention forms and experience crystallizes.

Dwelling from time to time in the experience of belonging to time can enliven life; it can augment your sense of how similar experiences of duration could issue in alternative turns or twists of life for other people; and it can expand the connections you pursue with others across cultural distance as you glimpse some forks in your own past. These claims, each encouraging the others without being determined entirely by them, will be met with skepticism by some. The fascinating thing is that argument and external evidence alone may not suffice to resolve the issue in either direction. *Running the experiment is the best way to test the claims.* It may be wise to run it before your brain has only six minutes left to think. It may be smart to run it a few times alone and then in the company of others whose creeds collide and collude with yours in one way or another. Watching illuminating films in the right mood is only one way to set such experiments into motion.

Different traditions become pertinent to engage at this point, depending in part upon the preliminary faith you bring to the experience of indwelling. Christianity, Islam, Judaism, Buddhism, Hinduism, and Nietzscheanism all have currents within them that focus on such practices. I myself am drawn to the explorations of Marcel Proust. He concurs with Bergson on the importance of indwelling. But more than Bergson, he teaches you how to make something of such an experiment as it begins to run itself. For such an event is not easy to choreograph in advance, as the dying man in *Waking Life* comes to realize.

Marcel needed a couple of fortuitous repetitions—in which he first slipped on some cobblestones and then heard the clatter of cutlery—to launch his experiment. An involuntary dimension of memory was tapped, one in which the repetition of an earlier sensory experience under new circumstances opened the floodgates to a larger wave of memory. Under this spell Marcel experienced vividly how waves of the past melt into the protraction of the present, enabling new experiences irreducible to memory as mere recollection or to simple repetition of the same: "But let a noise or a scent, once heard or once smelt, be heard or smelt again in the present and at the same time in the past, real without being actual, ideal without being abstract, and immediately the permanent and habitually concealed essence of things is liberated and our true self which seemed—had perhaps for years seemed—to be dead but which was not altogether dead, is awakened and reanimated as it receives the celestial nourishment that is brought to it. A minute freed from the order of time has re-created in us, to wit, the man freed from the order of time."[2]

To be freed from the order of time, on my reading, is to be released temporarily from the pressure of chrono-time and action; it is to become immersed in the qualitative multiplicity of a protracted present. Here a series of reverberations between first and second occasions engenders a vivid experience irreducible to either past or present understood as simple chronology. As Marcel puts it, "I experienced them at the present moment and at the same time in the context of a different moment, so that the past was made to encroach upon the present, and I was made to doubt whether I was in the one or the other."[3] Marcel calls such an experience "the only genuine pleasure I have known."[4] Some may suspect that this judgment signifies a lack in his sex life. But perhaps it is more insightful to say that sexual experience, if it moves you, also contains a moment freed from the order of chrono-time. It thereby speaks to a larger fund of temporal experience, rather than providing the single instance against which Marcel's experience is to be measured.

It is not only in *The Maltese Falcon*, *Waking Life*, *The Creative Mind*, or *Time Regained* that such experiences and testimony are encountered. Similar themes are advanced by Gilles Deleuze, as he explores "crystals of time" and appraises efforts by creative film directors to intensify "belief in this world" as a world of becoming.[5] And by Nietzsche and James too, as we glimpsed in earlier chapters. And by the Dalai Lama, as he probes experiences of living, dreaming, and dying.[6]

These figures do not agree on the details.[7] So much the better, in a pluralistic world that solicits multiple orientations to being and time. Moreover, I do not contend that dwelling in duration by itself always secures commitment to deep pluralism. Sometimes an uncanny event can press you in that direction. But, equally, sometimes a prior belief in the desirability of pluralism can be deepened and extended by dwelling in time. You can now cultivate a bicameral orientation to citizenship in which, for instance, *you* link the experience of belonging to time to finalism, while recoiling back modestly upon the self-certainty of your own judgment as you discern how a subtle twist here or there might have turned you in the direction *I* have taken; and *I* embrace the experience of time as becoming in an open universe while recoiling modestly back upon it as I sense how a minor turn here or there might have drawn me in the direction *you* now espouse. The experience of belonging to time can enliven the feeling for life and deepen appreciation of diversity at the same time.

I have been concentrating in this Postlude upon experiences that can enliven and ennoble you as you think, talk, argue, teach, or write about the attractions of pluralism, not so much upon the micropolitics through which larger assemblages are consolidated or the macropolitics by which state decisions are reached. The three dimensions are interconnected, of

course, as we have seen in previous chapters and as the collective recep-
tions of these films and books suggest. But the focus is now on the
individual as teacher, writer, student, and thinker.

But do the witnesses assembled here exaggerate? I am uncertain.
Even if so, the exaggerations may be useful during a time when some
theorists adopt shallow, secular models of diversity without attending to
the complexity of time and others engage the thickness of time only on
behalf of cultural nationalism. Commitment to democratic pluralism is
flat and tenuous to the extent that it is detached from the vitality of life;
regard for the thickness of time becomes narrow and stingy if confined
to pursuit of the nation. The idea, again, is to join the vivification of experience to the diversity of the human condition. The wager is that those
who run such experiments—through reading, testimony, and meditation, in concerts, theaters, temples, and other ritual settings—emerge
better prepared to respond with presumptive receptivity and courage to a
world that moves faster than heretofore and more often issues in surprising forks of time. We may also become better equipped to combat on
their own turf those who seek to roll the world back to a putative condition of deep unity and slow time. A preliminary commitment to deep,
multidimensional pluralism is amplified by the experience of belonging
to time.

NOTES

PRELUDE

1.   See T. W. Adorno, "Some Aspects of Religious Ideology . . ." and "Types and Syndromes" in Adorno, Else Frenkel-Brunswik, Daniel Levinson, and R. Nevitt Sanford, eds., *The Authoritarian Personality* (New York: W. W. Norton, 1950), 727–86.

2.   I first explored ways to reduce economic inequality in a mixed economy with Michael Best in *The Politicized Economy* (Lexington, Mass.: D. C. Heath, 1976, 1982). There we developed the distinction between exclusive modes of consumption and inclusive modes, supporting the latter in the domains of housing, travel, communication, insurance, and medical care. The unit costs of items in these domains decrease and the quality increases as they are extended more widely. The dominant mode of consumption today is exclusive goods. The difficulties in making ends meet grow as these goods become necessary items of consumption for more and more people. These themes are connected more closely to pluralism in chapter 3 of *The Ethos of Pluralization* (Minneapolis: University of Minnesota Press, 1995) and "Assembling the Left," *boundary 2*, fall 1999, 47–54. The latter essay appears in a symposium in which Paul Bove, Wendy Brown, Bruce Robbins, and Thomas Dumm speak eloquently to related issues.

CHAPTER 1: PLURALISM AND EVIL

1. Augustine, *Concerning the City of God: Against the Pagans*, trans. Henry Bettenson (Middlesex: Penguin, 1984), 14:571.

2. Augustine, *The Confessions*, trans. John K. Ryan (New York: Image, 1960), 9:205.

3. I consider these questions in detail in *The Augustinian Imperative: A Reflection on the Politics of Morality* (Newbury Park, Calif.: Sage, 1993; expanded edition New York: Rowman and Littlefield, 2001).

4. Augustine, *Select Letters*, trans. James H. Baxter (Cambridge: Harvard University Press, 1930), epistle 232.

5. Roxanne Euben, *Enemy in the Mirror: Islamic Fundamentalism and the Limits of Modern Rationalism* (Princeton: Princeton University Press, 1999), 63–64. Euben explores other Islamic clerics who do not embrace the extreme doctrine of Qutb. Her terms of comparison are between Islamic faith and western rationalism, arguing that the latter needs to become infused with deep meaning to avoid the alienation that accompanies it. My terms of comparison are between Qutbism and Augustinianism, issuing in a perspective that affirms a deep pluralism of faith to counter the problem of evil in the nexus between territory and faith. Euben's book can profitably be read with and against Talal Asad, *Formations of the Secular: Christianity, Islam, Modernity* (Stanford: Stanford University Press, 2003). That book is discussed in chapter 2.

6. In a very thoughtful essay entitled "The Indispensable Rival: William Connolly's Engagement with Augustine of Hippo," *Journal of the American Academy of Religion*, June 2004, 487–506, Kathleen Roberts Skerrett expresses appreciation of the rivalry that she charts. She also argues that while attention to Augustine on the divided will, evil, and heresy is important, there are positive resources to draw from his work, bound up in particular with his ideas of love and grace. I concur. Augustinian love is a positive source for Christians to draw upon in responding to the problem of evil within faith, discussed in the last part of this chapter. That love, however, will carry them into conflict with the other elements of the Augustinian creed.

7. See the discussion of 'Abduh in Euben, *Enemy in the Mirror*, 105–14. 'Abduh seems closer to Kant than to Augustine, as long as you treat Kant's "apodictic" recognition that morality takes the form of law to be a mystical experience operating below the threshold of conceptual experience.

8. See *The Book of J*, trans. David Rosenberg and interpreted by Harold Bloom (New York: Grove Weidenfeld, 1990).

9. *Spinoza: The Letters*, trans. Samuel Shirley (Indianapolis: Hackett, 1995), epistle 19.

10. I use the word "tolerance" here in awareness of the sense of superiority that it often conveys on the part of those who practice it. Agonistic respect, a reciprocal virtue of pluralist politics to be pursued later, diminishes this sense on both sides of the equation without perhaps eliminating it altogether. Spinoza was an advocate of tolerance, not agonistic respect. He favored the former because, as we shall see, he had inordinate confidence in the demonstrable superiority of an ethic of cultivation to those few who could grasp the complex arguments on its behalf.

11. *Spinoza: The Letters*, 135.

12. Ibid., 342.

13. Ibid.

14. For a rich history of the radical Enlightenment in Europe, the pivotal role Spinoza played in it, the harsh punishments meted out for a hundred years in Holland, France, Germany, and England to priests, theologians, and philosophers who either avowed Spinozism or were accused of it, and the ways in which the advent of Spinozism helped to create space for emergence of the "moderate Enlightenment," see Jonathan Israel, *Radical Enlightenment: Philosophy and the Making of Modernity, 1650–1750* (Oxford: Oxford University Press, 2001). Israel's book presents a micro-history of how power, thinking, and faith fold into one another, with many thinkers of the day seeking desperately to ward off charges that their philosophies and theologies were "Spinozist." For an essay that reviews this book, and probes sore spots in both the Spinozist and the Kantian ideas of reason, see my "The Radical Enlightenment: Faith, Power, Theory," *Theory and Event* 7, no. 3 (2004).

15. The relation between such traces and the idea of God, particularly as it emerges in the thought of Derrida, is explored in Hent de Vries, *Philosophy and the Turn to Religion* (Baltimore: Johns Hopkins University Press, 1999).

16. For a study that plays up the aesthetic imperative in the art of Picasso and the physics of Einstein, see Arthur I. Miller, *Einstein/Picasso: Space, Time and the Beauty That Causes Havoc* (New York: Basic Books, 2001). It is not, for instance, that Einstein's faith and image of beauty determined his theory. For others had a similar faith and did not devise the theory. But according to Miller, Einstein did not follow Heisenberg later because Heisenberg's "lack of classical imagery" and "violation of classical causality remained abhorrent to him" (258).

17. The point to note here is that what may be called radical difference or difference in itself is not the same as difference between an identity and contrasting identities. There are two dimensions of difference, visible difference in relation to an extant identity and difference in itself engendering real effects while subsisting below the level of conceptual articulation.

18. I pursue these themes in relation to the Rawlsian and Habermasian models

of secularism in *Why I Am Not a Secularist* (Minneapolis: University of Minnesota Press, 1999).

19. For two excellent studies that bring out the costs today of pursuing the impossible vision of the nation, see David Campbell, *National Deconstruction: Violence, Identity, and Justice in Bosnia* (Minneapolis: University of Minnesota Press, 1998), and Michael Shapiro, *Methods and Nations: Cultural Governance and the Challenge of the Arts* (New York: Routledge, 2004). Campbell charts how the refusal of pluralism in the former Yugoslavia issued in ethnic cleansing, effectively rebutting those who pretend that it is the "pursuit of difference" that produces such an effect. Shapiro extends the inquiry into the relations between settler societies and the indigenous populations who preceded them.

20. I explore this question in "The Liberal Image of the Nation," in Duncan Ivison, Paul Patton, and Will Sanders, eds., *Political Theory and the Rights of Indigenous Peoples* (Cambridge: Cambridge University Press, 2000), 183–98.

21. For a thoughtful elaboration of such a perspective see Judith Butler, *Bodies That Matter* (New York: Routledge, 1993). Patchen Markell, in *Bound by Recognition* (Princeton: Princeton University Press, 2003), argues that the attainment of "recognition" itself can be a form of entrapment. He pursues a politics of "acknowledgment" in which neither party to the relation demands a position of sovereignty.

22. The sort of experiments I have in mind have been run by V. S. Ramachandran with volunteers who report mystical experiences. See Ramachandran, *Phantoms in the Brain: Probing the Mysteries of the Human Mind* (New York: William Morrow, 1998), chapter 5. See also experiments with lucid dreaming reviewed in Francisco J. Varela, ed., *Sleeping, Dreaming and Dying: An Exploration of Consciousness with the Dalai Lama* (Boston: Wisdom, 1997).

23. Again, see Israel, *The Radical Enlightenment*, for a detailed account of what happened to each "Spinozist" uncovered in every European country during this period.

24. For an excellent review of the life and thought of Las Casas see Tzvetan Todorov, *The Conquest of America*, trans. Richard Howard (New York: Harper Colophon, 1982), chapter 3 and Epilogue. Other priests such as Sahagun are also important here.

CHAPTER 2: PLURALISM AND RELATIVISM

1. Leo Strauss, *Liberalism, Ancient and Modern* (Chicago: University of Chicago Press, 1968), 5.

2. Ibid., 36.

3. Ibid., 28.

4. Ibid.

5. Ibid., 31.

6. Ibid., 31, 34.

7. Ibid., 40.

8. Ibid., 40–41. For the persistence of this vocabulary in the representations of others by self-described "Straussians," see statement number 4 under "Some Distinguishing Aspects of a Straussian Approach to Political Philosophy," in Straussian.net: http://www2.bc.edu/7Ewilsonop/Straussianism.html, "A Recognition of the Dangers That Historicism, Relativism, Eclecticism, Scientism, and Nihilism Pose to Philosophy and Western Culture Generally . . ."

9. Ibid., 56–57.

10. Ibid., 63.

11. Ibid., 254.

12. Ibid., 254–55.

13. In a superb essay, "A Postmodern Return to Orthodoxy: Leo Strauss's Early Critique of Modern Liberalism," delivered at the fall 2003 convention of the American Political Science Association in Philadelphia, Miguel Vatter argues that Strauss's apparent commitment to classical reason above all is belied by his more basic commitment to Jewish orthodoxy. Drawing upon Strauss's early work, Vatter contends that he "envisages a return to orthodoxy that is both 'postmodern' and 'democratic' " (3). He also argues that Strauss's commitment to classical reason can be rendered compatible with such a movement, to the extent that Strauss displays the dependence of classical reason on faith. While impressed with Vatter's interpretation, I do not seek to decide whether Strauss is himself a believer or rather thinks most people must be believers in order to contain themselves and obey constituted authority. Whichever way it goes, Strauss's essay on Spinoza meshes well with an interpretation that Vatter develops from other sources.

14. William James, *The Will to Believe, and Other Essays in Popular Philosophy* (New York: Dover, 1956), x.

15. William J. Bennett, *Why We Fight: Moral Clarity and the War on Terrorism* (New York: Doubleday, 2002), 79.

16. Reported in Nicholas Kristof, http://forums.nytimes.com/webin/WebX?50@@.f3beae7 (17 August 2003).

17. Bennett, *Why We Fight*, 86.

18. The two dominant wings of the Enlightenment, on my reading, are the Spinozist and the Kantian.

19. Bennett, *Why We Fight*, 100.

20. Strauss, *Liberalism, Ancient and Modern*, 228.

21. Talal Asad, "Reading A Modern Classic: W. C. Smith's 'The Meaning and End of Religion,' " in Hent de Vries and Samuel Weber, eds., *Religion and the Media* (Stanford: Stanford University Press, 2001), 216.

22. Talal Asad, *Formations of the Secular* (Stanford: Stanford University Press, 2003), 38.

23. Ibid., 38–39.

24. Ibid., 55.

25. Ibid., 169.

26. Limits in my understandings of other places confine me here. But Gyanandra Pandey, in *Silencing the Present: History and the Homogenization of Contemporary India* (Cambridge: Cambridge University Press, forthcoming), applies a similar analysis and prescriptive orientation to the contemporary politics of India. He shows how the partition of Pakistan and India, organized around a religio-national imperative, intensified conflicts between Muslims and Hindus. And he pursues the possibility of a post-secular India that is pluralistic in shape.

27. As John Rawls puts it in one formulation, "We appeal to a political conception of justice to distinguish between those questions that can be reasonably removed from the political agenda and those that cannot. . . . To illustrate: from within a political conception of justice let us suppose we can account . . . for equal liberty of conscience, which takes the truths of religion off the agenda. . . . But by avoiding comprehensive doctrines we try to bypass religion and philosophy's profoundest controversies so as to have some hope of uncovering a stable consensus." *Political Liberalism* (Cambridge: Harvard University Press, 1993), 151–52. My engagement with Rawls on this and allied points is set forth in *Why I Am Not a Secularist* (Minneapolis: University of Minnesota Press, 1999), chapters 1 and 2.

28. I first emphasized the signal importance of multidimensional pluralism to the health of a polity in *Identity/Difference*, first published in 1991 and republished with a new preface in 2002 (Minneapolis: University of Minnesota Press). I did not see then the effect such a process could have on amplifying the experience of difference within faith practices. Etienne Balibar in *Politics and the Other Scene* (London: Verso, 2002) has very insightful things to say about the political effect of multiplying the types of minorities. He too, however, skips over the relation between this phenomenon and the amplification of difference within faith.

29. The language of multidimensional pluralism used here needs to be discussed in conjunction with the need to reduce the stratification of income, education, job security, and retirement prospects. I have argued elsewhere that pluralism and the reduction of inequality set conditions of possibility

for each other when each is pursued in the right way. I do not repeat that argument here. But its most recent formulations can be found in *The Ethos of Pluralization* (Minneapolis: University of Minnesota Press, 1995), chapter 3, and "Assembling the Left," *boundary 2*, fall 1999.

30. Asad comes to terms with this issue in Islam in *Genealogies of Religion*. In a very thoughtful book edited by Fabio Petito and Pavlos Hatzopoulos, *Religion in International Relations: The Return from Exile* (New York: Palgrave, 2003), several essays explore the effects of the Westphalian accord in privatizing religion and address this "site" as a potential source of connection across faiths. It is where they both resist secularism and transcend the quest for formation of an ecumenical creed that the essays make their most promising innovations. In that respect, the pieces by Scott Thomas, Cecelia Lynch, Carsten Bagge and Ole Waever, Richard Falk, and Fred Dallmayr are very thoughtful. The one limit is that few, if any, of these supporters of multiple orientations to transcendence concede the nobility that can reside in philosophy-faiths of radical immanence. A corrective to that omission, in a book which also explores the time in Spain when Christianity, Judaism, and Islam coexisted uneasily, is John Docker, *1492: The Poetics of Diaspora* (London: Continuum, 1999).

31. I in fact support what can be called a "double-entry orientation" to the universal. What this means becomes clear in chapter 4. For an exploration, which focuses on the advantages, complexities, and dangers of cultivating "distance" in ethico-political life, see Amanda Anderson, *The Powers of Distance* (Princeton: Princeton University Press, 2002).

32. When modern and postmodern secularists do focus on such practices one tendency is to define them as modes of manipulation to be transcended by intellectual effort. My argument, however, is that practices of rationality themselves involve disciplines and enactments that become embodied in the soft tissues of life, so that it now becomes a more complex matter to sort out manipulation from self-enactment. The issue haunts every social theory. The explorations of critical responsiveness and agonistic respect later in this book speak to this issue.

CHAPTER 3: PLURALISM AND THE UNIVERSE

1. William James, *A Pluralistic Universe* (Lincoln: University of Nebraska Press, 1996), 40. I note that my interest in James has been spurred by conversations with Richard Flathman. His discussion of James in *Willful Liberalism: Voluntarism and Individuality in Political Theory and Practice* (Ithaca: Cornell University Press, 1992) is thoughtful and provocative.

2. James, *A Pluralistic Universe*, 34.

3. For an essay which explores the agentic capacities of human and nonhuman assemblages, see Jane Bennett, "The Force of Things: Steps toward an Ecology of Matter," *Political Theory*, June 2004, 347–72.
4. James, *A Pluralistic Universe*, 45.
5. Ibid., 321.
6. Ibid., 36.
7. Ibid., 232.
8. Ibid., 254.
9. Ibid., 263.
10. Ibid., 283.
11. Ibid., 277.
12. Ibid., 313.
13. Ibid., 29.
14. See *The Book of J*, trans. David Rosenberg and interpreted by Harold Bloom (New York: Grove Weidenfeld, 1990).
15. James, *A Pluralistic Universe*, 311.
16. Ibid., 299.
17. Ibid., 328.
18. Ibid., 328.
19. Ibid., 329.
20. Ibid., 330.
21. These themes are developed in Ilya Prigogine, *The End of Certainty: Time, Chaos and the New Laws of Nature* (New York: Free Press, 1996).
22. Isabelle Stengers, *Power and Invention* (Minneapolis: University of Minnesota Press, 1997), 10–11.
23. Stephen Wolfram, *A New Kind of Science* (Champaign: Wolfram Media, 2002), 28.
24. Ibid.
25. Ibid., 741.
26. Brian Goodwin, *How the Leopard Changed Its Spots: The Evolution of Complexity* (Princeton: Princeton University Press, 2001), particularly the last two chapters.
27. Wolfram, *A New Kind of Science*, 545.
28. See Lynn Margulis and Dorion Sagan, *Microcosmos* (London: Allen and Unwin, 1987), as well as the more recent book by them, *What Is Life?* (Berkeley: University of California Press, 1995). As they present evolution writ large in the second book, it "is no mechanical law but a complex of processes, sensitive and symbiogenetic, in part resulting from the choices and actions of evolving organic beings themselves . . . Nature is no black box but a kind of sentient symphony" (164).
29. William James, "The Dilemma of Determinism," in John J. McDermott, ed.,

The Writings of William James (Chicago: University of Chicago Press, 1977), 591.

30. Manuel De Landa, *A Thousand Years of Nonlinear History* (New York: Zone, 2001), 64. A comparison could be made between on the one hand De Landa's reading of lava flows and granite formations and on the other the reading of ordinary life given by Thomas Dumm in *The Politics of the Ordinary* (New York: New York University Press, 1999).

31. See Jane Bennett, *The Enchantment of Modern Life* (Princeton: Princeton University Press, 2001). This book sparkles with examples of the sort listed above.

32. Henri Bergson, *Creative Evolution*, trans. Arthur Mitchell (New York: Dover, 1998), 106.

INTERLUDE

1. William James, *A Pluralistic Universe* (Lincoln: University of Nebraska Press, 1996), 328.

2. Leo Strauss, *Liberalism, Ancient and Modern* (Chicago: University of Chicago Press, 1968), 254.

3. Ibid, 254–55.

4. James, *A Pluralistic Universe*, 45.

5. Ibid., 34.

6. Ibid., 254.

7. Isabelle Stengers, *Power and Invention* (Minneapolis: University of Minnesota Press, 1997), 10–11.

8. James, *A Pluralistic Universe*, 328.

9. Henri Bergson, *Creative Evolution*, trans. Arthur Mitchell (New York: Dover, 1998), 106.

10. Proust, *Time Regained*, vol. 3 of *Remembrance of Things Past*, trans. C. K. Scott Moncrief (New York: Vintage, 1981), 905.

CHAPTER 4: PLURALISM AND TIME

1. In "Reclaiming Mind, Body and Cognition," in Walter J. Freeman and Rafael Núñez, eds., *Reclaiming Cognition: The Primacy of Action, Intention, and Emotion* (Thorverton: Imprint Academic, 1999), the neuroscientist Rafael Núñez poses numerous such suggestions and shows the habit of expressing temporal relations in spatial terms to be very common cross-culturally. The upshot of his article is that neuroscientists need to pay more attention to embodied orientations to practice than they have in the past.

2. Experiments with infrasound are increasingly common in contemporary neuroscience. In one set, reported in the *Guardian* on 8 September 2003, the researchers "played an experimental organ pipe too low to be heard and

then collected reports of strange reactions—sorrow, coldness, anxiety and shivers down the spine." The experiment was double blind. It studied those vibrations in organ music which fall below the threshold of hearing but within the threshold of vibrations that could be sensed unconsciously.

3. Henri Bergson, *The Creative Mind: An Introduction to Metaphysics*, trans. Mabelle L. Andison (New York: Philosophical Library, 1946), 163.

4. Ibid., 162.

5. Ibid., 179.

6. Bergson, *Creative Evolution*, trans. Arthur Mitchell (New York: Dover, 1998), 339. Bergson's theory of evolution has several affinities to the image of evolution supported in complexity theory today; both emphasize the creative element in evolution. But the connection to Bergson is typically unattended to because of his concept of *élan vital*, an impetus that is treated by biologists as too spiritual in origin and shape to fit into complexity theory. For an excellent account that calls attention to the similarities, repositions *élan vital*, and explores complexity as duration, see Robin Durie, "Creativity and Life," *Review of Metaphysics*, December 2002, 357–83. The contemporary biologists engaged in that piece are Stuart Kauffman and Brian Goodwin.

7. I explore this side of Nietzsche's thought in chapter 6 of *Neuropolitics: Thinking, Culture, Speed* (Minneapolis: University of Minnesota Press, 2002).

8. Bergson, *Creative Evolution*, 343.

9. Ibid., 339.

10. I develop a concept of emergent causation in "Method, Problem, Faith," in Ian Shapiro, Rogers M. Smith, and Tarek E. Masoud, eds., *Problems and Methods in the Study of Politics* (Cambridge: Cambridge University Press, 2004).

11. It is relevant to see that Ilya Prigogine, whose conception of natural science we reviewed in the last chapter, concurs that becoming is the mode assumed by time not only in human culture but also in those natural systems that are "out of equilibrium." As he says, "Our universe is far from equilibrium, non-linear and full of irreversible processes . . . We see stars being born, other stars die and all kinds of non-equilibrium structures, but we do not understand how the universe remains far from equilibrium." *Is Future Given* (London: World Scientific, 2003). He agrees with Bergson, in opposition to classical physicists, that the arrow of time is real, irreversible, and carries alteration and novelty with it. His debt to Bergson on these points, including the idea that it is wise to proceed from the human experience of duration to speculation about time, can be found on pages 60–61 of the same book.

12. Bergson, *The Two Sources of Morality and Religion*, trans. R. Ashley Audra and Cloudesley Brereton, with the assistance of W. Horsfall Carter (New York: Henry Holt, 1934), 256.

13. Friedrich Nietzsche, *The Will To Power*, ed. Walter Kaufmann, trans. Walter Kaufmann and R. J. Hollingdale (New York: Vintage, 1968), n. 1067. This note, and much else that Nietzsche writes, poses the question of the relation between his doctrine of the immanence of "becoming" or "will to power" and the equally adamant idea of "eternal return." One way to render the two consistent is to treat the only published version, developed in *Thus Spoke Zarathustra*, as definitive. There return can be interpreted as the eternal return of the creative dissonance of the moment, that gateway out of which alteration eternally springs. I pursue such a reading in *Neuropolitics*, chapter 6. Another reading, perhaps more congruent with note 1067, quoted in the text, is to set the creativity of becoming in huge cycles of time that return endlessly, "with tremendous years of recurrence" (same note). But those cycles, however long, seem to subtract creativity from the alterations within each cycle. To sustain creativity you would need a theory that says that each cycle of recurrence, however long, follows a course that differs from those preceding it. I embrace Nietzschean ideas of becoming while resisting a notion of cycles that return endlessly.

14. Bergson, *The Two Sources of Morality and Religion*, 262. The difference between Bergson and Nietzsche here finds some expression in that the first believes in an afterlife of some sort, while the second, depending on how you read eternal return, treats death either as oblivion or as an end that will, after a tremendously long cycle, reissue in the individual. But there would be no memory of being reissued.

15. Ibid., 267.

16. For an excellent account of trauma time see Jenny Edkins, *Trauma and the Memory of Politics* (Cambridge: Cambridge University Press, 2003). As she says, trauma time is the "disruptive, back to front time that occurs when the smooth time of the imagined or symbolic story is interrupted by the real of events." It is the "time that must be forgotten if the sovereign power of the modern state is to remain unchallenged." (229–30). Survivors of trauma often seek to stop the state from taking it over. You might also compare the inversion that marks trauma time to a less intense variant, in which you first experience a thud in your stomach and then, a half-second later, your intelligence catches up to record explicitly the worry that had been registered in the thud. Here the retrospective tendency is to recall the reflection as if it came first and the thud second, when it is actually the other way round. For a sophisticated account of the half-second delay and the corollary drive to obscure it see Brian Massumi, *Parables For the Virtual* (Durham: Duke University Press, 2002).

17. Proust, *Time Regained*, vol. 3 of *Remembrance of Things Past*, trans. C. K. Scott Moncrieff (New York: Vintage, 1981), 905.

18. *Religion within the Limits of Reason Alone*, trans. Theodore Greene and Hoyt Hudson (New York: Harper, 1934), 61.

19. I have discussed the differences between these two sources of morality and ethics elsewhere, in the preface to the new edition of *Identity/Difference* (New York: Rowman and Littlefield, 2002).

20. Bergson, *The Two Sources of Morality and Religion*, 99.

21. Immanuel Kant, *Critique of Practical Reason*, ed. and trans. Lewis Beck (New York: Macmillan, 1993), 79.

22. Bergson, *The Two Sources of Morality and Religion*, 230.

23. It would be pertinent to engage more closely the debate between philosophies of abundance-difference on one side and those of transcendence-otherness on the other. I start that discussion in *Neuropolitics*, chapters 4–5. In Mary Bryden, ed., *Deleuze and Religion* (London: Routledge, 2001), Daniel Smith reviews some of the salient issues in a very thoughtful way in chapter 13. So do Philip Goodchild and Keith Ansell Pearson in chapters 11 and 12. Nathan Widder's study *Genealogies of Difference* (Urbana: University of Illinois Press, 2002) reviews the history of these debates in an exemplary way.

24. I have explored particular examples of how such tactics work in *Neuropolitics*, particularly chapters 4–6.

CHAPTER 5: PLURALISM AND SOVEREIGNTY

1. Justice Souter's opinion is quoted in its entirety in the *New York Times*, 14 December 2000, 28–29. The quotation from Souter in the next paragraph comes from page 29 too.

2. Rousseau, *On the Social Contract: With Geneva Manuscript and Political Economy*, trans. Judith Masters (New York: St Martin's, 1978), 1:46. A thoughtful and detailed engagement of its role in Rousseau's theory is developed by Steven Johnston in *Encountering Tragedy: Rousseau and the Project of Democratic Order* (Ithaca: Cornell University Press, 1999). Johnston brings out how Rousseau developed an extensive theory of "governmentality" and "micropolitics" well before Foucault and Deleuze popularized the two themes.

3. See the discussion of the indeterminacy of language, rule, and law in Rousseau in Connolly, *Political Theory and Modernity* (Oxford: Basil Blackwell, 1988), 53–57. That section is also where I explore the paradox of founding in Rousseau for the first time.

4. Rousseau, *On the Social Contract*, 69–70.

5. Giorgio Agamben, *Homo Sacer: Sovereign Power and Bare Life*, trans. Daniel Heller-Roazen (Stanford: Stanford University Press, 1995), 82.

6. Ibid., 83.

7. Ibid., 44, 59.

8. This story is brilliantly told in Hans Blumenberg, *The Legitimacy of the Modern Age* (Cambridge: MIT Press, 1983).

9. Alexis de Tocqueville, *Democracy in America*, trans. George Lawrence (New York: Harper and Row, 1969), 58.

10. Tocqueville, *Democracy in America*, 336. I explore Tocqueville's rendering of the relation between the Christian civilization of America and Amerindians who were excluded by it in *The Ethos of Pluralization* (Minneapolis: University of Minnesota Press, 1995), chapter 6.

11. Tocqueville, *Democracy in America*, 294.

12. Gilles Deleuze and Felix Guattari, *A Thousand Plateaus*, trans. Brian Massumi (Minneapolis: University of Minnesota Press, 1987), 214.

13. Chantal Mouffe examines ambiguities in Schmitt's conception of the exception and the sovereign decision in *The Democratic Paradox* (New York: Verso, 2000), chapter 2. She too thinks that Schmitt's focus on the exception and the decision becomes problematical when you come to terms with his prior commitment to decisions that enforce, as she calls it, "homogeneity." To relax that latter demand is to set the stage to renegotiate the ethos of sovereignty. A compelling engagement with the paradox of sovereignty can be found in Bonnie Honig, *Democracy and the Foreigner* (Princeton: Princeton University Press, 2001). Honig focuses on the creative role of the foreigner in responding to the gap between law and sovereign power.

14. In a thoughtful essay Mark Wenman compares Chantal Mouffe, James Tully, and me on the question of pluralism and the constitution. While appreciating the place that pluralization, as the emergence of new identities, rights, and practices, plays in my conception, he finds me to be "naive" and "optimistic" in expecting a generous ethos to arise. He looks rather to "constitutional rules of the game" to limit sovereign exclusions. But both optimism and pessimism are spectatorial views, when what is needed is active involvement in a politics that seeks to build pluralism into the ethos of sovereignty, whether you are "optimistic" about the probability of success or not. Moreover, given the turns of time, no set of constitutional rules is self-determining. Furthermore, as in the case of the Amerindians reviewed above, a court may rule in favor of pluralism and be overruled by vigilantes, or a militaristic president, or a racist police force, or all three in conjunction. I present a generous ethos of engagement as a possibility to pursue, not a predicted probability. When the paradox of sovereignty yawns a pluralist is *presumptively* inclined toward the inclusive decision, whereas a Schmittian—which Wenman is not— solicits military-executive action on behalf of unity, narrowly defined. Both actions might be consistent with constitutionalism, depending on the ethos that infuses it. See Wenman's " 'Agonistic Pluralism' and Three Archetypal Forms of Politics," *Contemporary Political Theory*, fall 2003, 165–86.

15. In an earlier essay I develop a different counterexample to Hardt's and Negri's celebration of transformation by the "multitude" than that pursued in this piece. There it is the cross-state politics of indigenous peoples; here it will be a cross-state citizen activism which speaks to the Israeli-Palestinian conflict. For the first account see Connolly, "The Complexity of Sovereignty," in Jenny Edkins and Michael Shapiro, eds., *Sovereign Lives: Power in Global Politics* (Oxford: Macmillan, 2005), 23–40.

16. Michael Hardt and Antonio Negri, *Empire* (Cambridge: Harvard University Press, 2000), xiv. A more detailed summary of this structure is presented on pages 309–10.

17. Hardt and Negri, *Empire*, 181.

18. See Ian Angus, "Empire, Borders, Place: A Critique of Hardt and Negri's concept of Empire," *Theory and Event* 7, no. 3 (2004). Angus argues, first, that the United States is more the an imperial power than a state at the narrow pinnacle of empire and, second, that Hardt and Negri do not appreciate how countries such as Canada, separated by a border from the United States, can experiment with possibilities that eventually put pressure upon the imperial power. I think that Angus is partly right in his first critique. But he underplays the global effects of capital. He makes an important point in his focus on the continuing role of borders. I will discuss the potential power of cross-border citizen movements rendered possible by the global dimension of sovereignty. A focus on the resilience of borders complements rather than contradicts that analysis.

19. Hardt and Negri, *Empire*, 31.

20. Ibid., 157.

21. Ibid., 314.

22. There are, of course, multiple readings of Marx. For example the presentation and revision of Marxist materialism found in chapter 4 of Wendy Brown's *Politics out of History* (Princeton: Princeton University Press, 2001) resonates with the position attributed to Deleuze here. This is a book, indeed, from which a creative interchange between Deleuze and Marx could begin.

23. I presented an earlier version of this chapter on a panel at the convention of the American Political Science Association in the fall of 2002. Michael Hardt responded. He further clarified some aspects of the theory presented in the book, but he remained adamant about the multitude as the transformative force.

24. Hardt and Negri, *Empire*, 205, 214, 204, 411.

25. In a thoughtful review of *Empire* in *Theory and Event* Kam Shapiro writes, "The Multitude thus operates in Hardt's and Negri's narrative as the engine of historical change, a de-territorializing force of 'liberation' around which the powers of sovereignty reactively coalesce but which they never manage

to arrest . . . In seeking to invest itself in the biopolitical realm, therefore, Sovereignty is always tending towards its limit at a deeper threshold of difference and instability." "From Dream to Desire: At the Threshold of Old and New Utopias," *Theory and Event* 4, no. 4 (2000). This summary exposes an ambiguity in the idea of the multitude in need of further work: (a) its use to mark multiple points of energy, resistance, and creativity that exceed the governing power of Empire, and (b) its identification as a quasi constituency able to transform Empire. It is when you come to terms with that which is positive in the porous assemblage of Empire that the potential to move Empire by militant but nonrevolutionary means becomes credible.

26. Hardt, "Sovereignty," *Theory and Event* 5, no. 4 (2002).

27. This chapter was first composed in the summer of 2002, before the "coalition" invasion of Iraq. That invasion, besides imposing massive suffering on civilians and young American and Iraqi soldiers, disconnects the United States from supranational institutions, misidentifies the sources of terrorism, foments new terrorist energies, and delays further the day when a state of Palestine is formed to coexist with Israel.

28. For two essays which contend that the situation on the ground, particularly the pattern of Sharon's settlements in the occupied territories, requires a one-state response, see Eyal Weizman, "The Politics of Verticality," and Rafi Segal and Eyal Weisman, "The Battle for the Hilltops," in Anselm Franke, ed., *Territories* (Berlin: Institute For Contemporary Art, 2003), 65–118, 119–50. Each alternative needs debate, and each carries danger. A one-state response does not, even if enacted, guarantee real equality of citizenship on the ground, and a two-state response, while showing promise to relieve the worst suffering in the present, could create a volatile mixture of its own. Either is better than the current situation.

29. Uri Ram, "From Nation-State to Nation: State, Nation, History and Identity Struggles in Jewish Israel," in Ephraim Nimni, ed., *The Challenge of Post-Zionism* (London: Zed, 2003), 31–33. The essays by Ilan Pappe, Ephraim Nimni, Hannah Herzog, and Edward Said in this volume all speak to the history of the Israeli-Palestinian issue in reflective ways.

30. Michel Foucault, "Practicing Criticism," in Lawrence Kritzman, ed., *Michel Foucault: Politics, Philosophy, Culture*, trans. Alan Sheridan (New York: Routledge, 1988), 156.

POSTLUDE: BELONGING TO TIME

1. Henri Bergson, *The Creative Mind: An Introduction to Metaphysics*, trans. Mabelle L. Andison (New York: Philosophical Library, 1946), 157.

2. Marcel Proust, *Time Regained*, vol. 3 of *Remembrance of Things Past*, trans. C. K. Scott Moncrieff (New York: Vintage, 1981), 906.

3.   Ibid., 904.

4.   Ibid., 908.

5.   See Deleuze, *Cinema II: The Time Image*, trans. Hugh Tomlinson and Robert Galeta (New York: Athlone, 1989), 164–88.

6.   See the exchanges between the Dalai Lama and neuroscientists in Francesco Varela, ed., *Sleeping, Dreaming and Dying: An Exploration of Consciousness with the Dalai Lama* (Boston: Wisdom, 1997).

7.   For example, Proust may think that the reverberations that constitute duration move you close to an experience of timelessness as eternity, as when he says "that the contemplation, though it was of eternity, has been fugitive." *Time Regained*, 908. Bergson, on the other hand, tends to treat time as continuous alteration, while Nietzsche is more attuned to the periodic leaps through which new twists and turns emerge.

INDEX

'Abduh, Muhammed, 19, 27
aboriginal peoples, 30
Abu Ghraib, 137
abundance, 75, 124–25, 182 n. 23
activism, sites of, 7, 154–58
Adorno, Theodor, 4
affect, 90–91
Agamben, Giorgio, 10; on bare life, 14; on sovereignty, 136–40, 143
agency, in nature, 6, 72, 88
agonistic respect: agony of, 33, 123–24, 125; Augustine and, 16; courage and, 81; James and, 80–82; Spinoza and, 24–25; tolerance and, 125, 173 n. 10; virtue of, 31, 47, 49, 64, 123–26, 147
Al Qaeda, 6, 50, 53, 154, 155
All That Heaven Allows (film), 113–14
Americanism, 49–54
Amerindians, 12, 30, 142–44

Amnesty International, 150
Anderson, Amanda, 177 n. 31
Angus, Ian, 184 n. 18
anxiety, 104, 108, 163
Aquinas, Thomas, 141
Arendt, Hannah, 118
Asad, Talal, 10; on Islam, 55–59; on secularism, 55–59; sensibility of, 57
assemblage, Left, 9
atheism, 19, 57, 63. *See also* nontheism
attunement, 107
Augustine, 10; on Bible, 20, 78; on confession, 58; on evil, 14–19, 21; faith and, 27; Manicheanism and, 15–16; mystery and, 62, 118; transcendence and, 46; will and, 15
autopoiesis, 103

Balibar, Etienne: on minorities, 176 n. 28

William E. Connolly is the Krieger-Eisenhower Professor of Political Science at Johns Hopkins University. He is the author of many books, including *Neuropolitics: Thinking, Culture, and Speed* (2002), *The Ethos of Pluralization* (1995), and *Identity/Difference: Democratic Negotiations of Political Paradox* (1991).

Library of Congress Cataloging-in-Publication Data
Connolly, William E.
Pluralism / William Connolly.
p. cm.
Includes bibliographical references and index.
ISBN 0-8223-3554-9 (cloth : alk. paper)
ISBN 0-8223-3567-0 (pbk. : alk. paper)
1. Pluralism (Social sciences)—Political aspects.
2. Pluralism (Social sciences)—United States. 3. Toleration.
I. Title.
HM1271.C656 2005
323.1′01—dc22   2004030132